John Lockwood

Our Campaign around Gettysburg

Being a Memorial of what was endured, suffered, and accomplished by the

Twenty-third Regiment

John Lockwood

Our Campaign around Gettysburg
Being a Memorial of what was endured, suffered, and accomplished by the Twenty-third Regiment

ISBN/EAN: 9783337192839

Printed in Europe, USA, Canada, Australia, Japan

Cover: Foto ©ninafisch / pixelio.de

More available books at **www.hansebooks.com**

OUR CAMPAIGN

AROUND

GETTYSBURG:

BEING

A MEMORIAL OF WHAT WAS ENDURED, SUFFERED
AND ACCOMPLISHED BY THE

Twenty-Third Regiment

(N. Y. S. N. G.,)

AND

OTHER REGIMENTS ASSOCIATED WITH THEM, IN THEIR
PENNSYLVANIA AND MARYLAND CAMPAIGN,

DURING THE

Second Rebel Invasion of the Loyal States

IN JUNE—JULY, 1863.

"Quaeque ipse miserrima vidi,
Et quorum pars * * * fui"

Brooklyn:
A. H. ROME & BROTHERS, STATIONERS AND PRINTERS.
No. 383 Fulton Street.

1864.

PREFACE.

If any one, taking up this book casually, should wonder why it was written, it may suffice to observe that "Gettysburg" is probably destined to mark an Epoch of the Republic;—as being one of the very few decisive battles of the Great Rebellion. Accordingly, whosoever took any part in it may hope to share its immortality of glory.

But, says one, the militia were not engaged in the battle. True; neither was the reserve of eleven thousand men, under General French, at Frederick and elsewhere. Yet who would withhold from these veterans the honor of having been participators in the great struggle? They had their part to play—not so direct, nor conspicuous, nor important a part as they played whose valor won the day, yet important withal. Enough for the militia, they offered their lives for the Fatherland, and stood instant, waiting only for orders to hurry into the front of battle.

To the militia force, mainly of the cities of New York and Brooklyn, was from the first entrusted the defence of the valley of the Susquehanna. The Army of the Potomac could afford no protection to Harrisburg and the rich agricultural regions lying around it. For General Hooker, notwithstanding his vigilance and activity, had not prevented the advance corps of the enemy, under General Ewell, from penetrating to the very banks of the Susquehanna. Whether or not he cared to prevent it, is not here considered. A little later, to be sure, Lee became evidently alarmed on account of his extended line and made haste to contract it. But during the few days of panic that intervened between the first appearance of the enemy along the Susquehanna and their hasty departure therefrom, nothing stood between them and Harrisburg save the militia, whom General Halleck in his Official Report reviewing the military operations of the year 1863, saw fit to allude to as follows:—

"Lee's army was supposed to be advancing against Harrisburg, which was garrisoned by State militia, upon which little or no reliance could be placed."

York had fallen; and, notwithstanding the Mayor of that city — be his name forever buried in oblivion — went out to meet the enemy hoping doubtless to secure his favor by craven submission, a heavy ransom had been exacted for its exemption from pillage. A rebel detachment had fallen upon and put to flight the force guarding the bridge over the Susquehanna at Columbia, and thus compelled the burning of that fine structure ; while Ewell with the main body of his corps was moving cautiously up toward Harrisburg. Finally, when within five miles of Bridgeport Heights, having driven in the force of skirmishers who—militia, be it observed —had for several days gallantly held in check the head of the advancing column, he halted. The state capital was a tempting prize, but scarcely worth to him the risk of a desperate battle. The gates of the city were shut, and Ewell hesitated to hurl his masses against them. It is not now pertinent to enquire what might have resulted had he chosen to attack. He did not attack, and the capital of Pennsylvania was spared the shame of having to pass beneath the yoke of a conqueror. To the militia of New York and Brooklyn, in the main, is due the praise of having saved her that humiliation.

The reason which prompted this bold and enterprising commander to observe unusual circumspection in his advance up the Cumberland Valley is obvious. He held the extreme right of the rebel line, whose left could not have been much short of fifty miles distant. The militia of Pennsylvania, Ohio, New Jersey and New York, had been summoned in haste to the border, and for ten days they had been pouring down in unknown numbers. Thus Ewell found himself confronted by an unreckoned host, whose numbers would naturally, by one in his exposed situation, be magnified. The position of defence was a strong one, and to have failed in an assault upon it might easily have involved his destruction, and, as a consequence, the destruction of the whole rebel army. Could he have had a day or two longer to enable him to gain correct information of the strength of the works, and of the garrison, he would not probably have hesitated to attempt the capture of the place. But the action of the great drama was now moving forward with startling rapidity. Meade was concentrating on the flank of Lee, who saw that not a day was to be lost in distant and secondary expeditions. Ewell was accordingly recalled with all haste; and happy had it been for the Union cause had the General commanding the Department of the Susquehanna been early enough apprised of the hurried withdrawal of the enemy to make the services of the militia available at Gettysburg.

But the defence of Harrisburg, which was the main objective of General Lee in his raid up the Susquehanna Valley, is not the only title which the New York Militia hold to the gratitude of Pennsylvania and of the Nation. Who shall undertake to say how far the result of the battle of Gettysburg was determined by the fact of Union militia reinforcements being near at hand — their strength vastly over-estimated, there is no doubt, by both armies? Indeed there was reason to suppose, and many believed, while the battle was raging, that they had already come up and were actually engaged. The moral effect of such a report circulated through the ranks of contending forces, and even half credited, is immense. The one it fills with enthusiasm and animates to heroic endurance, for it summons them to victory; the other it fills with terror, and makes effort seem useless, for it is to them the omen of coming defeat. Nevertheless there can be little doubt that at the close of the third day of conflict the rebel army was still a powerful host—its organization not irreparably broken, its numbers equal if not, indeed, superior to those opposed to it. True, it had been repulsed with terrible slaughter, but it was far from being vanquished, for it was made up of hardy and oft victorious veterans, to whom repulse was not defeat. General Meade did not feel strong enough to assume the offensive; and who shall undertake to say that there had yet arisen an imperious necessity for the withdrawal of Lee across the Potomac, except as involved in this very matter of reinforcements?

With regard to the ungenerous disparagement contained in the remarks of General Halleck it is quite likely that he merely meant to say that the troops hurriedly collected at Harrisburg were untried, and therefore ought not to be entrusted with any critical service. But the words, as they stand, carry with them a sweeping detraction and are nothing less than calumnious. The Brooklyn Twenty-Third — or rather the Division, taken as a whole, with which it was incorporated — has only to point to its record as given very imperfectly in the following History, and especially to the farewell orders of General Meade, and of the commander of the Division, Brigadier General W. F. Smith, to whom the nation is now looking as a military chieftain of great promise, for a vindication of its fair name.

But it is not on account of any supposed historic value attaching to the story it tells, that this book has been written. It was undertaken rather as a memorial of the campaign of the Twenty-Third Regiment and of other regiments with which it was from time to time associated, interesting chiefly to the men who participated in the events described, and to their friends. These will find herein a portraiture, faithful so far as it goes, of the daily life they led amid the monotony of the camp, the excitement of the siege, the perpetual worry of the bivouac; of the martial achievements they performed, and some they narrowly escaped performing; in a word, of the sum total of the services they rendered to the Nation during those momentous Thirty Days.

The statistics of the book have been compiled with care and fidelity. The distances of that part of the line of march which lay in Cumberland, Adams and Franklin counties, Pennsylvania, have been measured off carefully on elaborate county maps, kindly loaned for the purpose by Colonel Everdell. For the remainder of the route, no similar guides being accessible, only approximate results were attainable. If any one is disappointed to find these distances shorter than his own rough estimates, he is reminded that the reckoning is made in those tantalizing "Pennsylvania" miles — probably the longest on the globe — with which we became so painfully familiar.

Having for the sake of the general reader scrupulously avoided throughout the following narrative all allusions of a merely private or personal interest, I should be wanting in good feeling, were I to let this opportunity pass without paying my respects to those of my companions in arms, to whom I am indebted for friendship, for kindness and for sympathy. I am the more incited to make this acknowledgment from the belief that I am not alone in cherishing such grateful recollections — that many a heart will respond tenderly to all I shall say.

Who of my company can soon forget the tender solicitude of Acting Captain Shepard for his men — on the march, helping the weary by bearing their burdens at the expense of his own strength, itself delicate; at the bivouac, providing suitable care for the sick; and ever prompt to spend himself for his command in a hundred delicate and unnoticed ways? Or, the intelligent activity of Acting First Lieutenant Van Ingen, the thorough disciplinarian and dashing officer; to whose energy and forethought the company were primarily indebted, at the end of many a hard day's march, for an early cup of hot coffee, and a bed of rails which otherwise had been a bed of mud ! Nor should I do justice to my emotions did I fail to bear record to the prudence and sagacity of Acting Second Lieutenant Hunter, whose dignity of character, finely blended with genial humor, at once commanded the respect and secured the attachment of his men; who was watchful against danger and cool in the midst of it; who knew his duty as a soldier and loyally discharged it, however distasteful it might sometimes be to himself or his command.

Nor can I forget the genial and capable Sergeant-Major Ogden, as ready to surrender his horse to a foot-sore soldier as to cheer the drooping spirits of his company by his patriotic and exuberant singing while " marching along "; Dr. Bennett, the amiable and popular Assistant Surgeon ; Story, the ever-punctual and faithful Orderly, who had the art to soften distasteful requirements by a gentlemanly suavity ; Sergeant Blossom, self-respecting and respected, perpetually finding something to do to render the general hardships more endurable, and going about it with so little ostentation that it too often passed unappreciated ; Hazard, genial, impulsive, generous ; Howland, who, on the march, bore the heaviest burden with the least murmuring; and with exemplary fidelity was ever to be found in his place as the guide of the company, plodding along unfalteringly ; Corporal Hurlbut, snatching from an exhausted comrade the musket which was dragging him down, to bear it upon his own weary shoulders; Thornton, whose common sense and merry wit and kindly disposition gave him an entrance to every heart; Allen, modest, amiable, faithful in duty; Deland, with a heart big enough to contain the regiment; Van Ingen, tender of sympathies as a girl, and strong in every manly virtue; now greeting with kindly recognition some neglected and unnoticed soldier; now helping another to bear his burden, though struggling wearily under his own.

Green be the memory, too, of Shick, who kept the pot boiling while the rest slept, on many and many a dismal night, that they might have cooked rations for the morrow's journey; and Wales, the intelligent counsellor; and Stevens, spirited, attentive, generous, and a model of personal tidiness; and Hubbell, who hid beneath a mask of indifference a warm and generous heart; and Lockwood, the upright, trusty and solid soldier; and Palmer and Johnson and Burr — members of the regiment only during the campaign — who won the praise of all by their affable manners and their assiduity in whatsoever capacity. And finally, I greet with grateful remembrance thee, O youthful Hood, whose winning manners early gave thee the key to my heart; and thee, Oliver, handsome as Apollo and a thousand times more useful, the mirror of virtue and refinement, whose praises were on every lip for every soldierly quality.

Would that I might add to this pleasing roll of personal acquaintance and friendship the names of others of my comrades, as genial, true and gallant, doubtless, as the regiment affords, but whom it was not my happiness to know.

I must content myself, in closing these prefatory remarks, with expressing my thankfulness for having been permitted to share in a glorious service with as noble and gallant a regiment as ever offered itself, a free sacrifice, on the altar of Country and Liberty.

It is due to the Twenty-Third Regiment that I should not conclude without observing that the memorial which follows is not in any sense to be considered as representing that regiment. Having been connected with the Twenty-Third only during its absence, it would be simply a piece of impertinence in me to claim to speak for it. And this very circumstance of being an outsider has given me an advantage. For, unconscious of any motive except to tell the truth and render praise where I believed it to be due, I have felt at liberty to say many things which modesty would have forbidden a member to say, as well as some things which one representing the regiment might have thought had better been left unspoken. I have aimed to give, simply, truthfully, the story of the life we led, in all its lights and shadows, as far as my limited opportunities furnished the materials.

I.

OFF TO THE WAR.

The Pennsylvania Governor, Curtin, cried to us for help; the President called out from the White House that he wanted us to come down to the Border; our Governor, Seymour, said go, and accordingly we hurriedly kissed those we loved best, and started for the wars. Let us look at the record in order:—

Monday, June 15th.—News comes that the rebel General Lee is on the march for the free States. The President issues a Proclamation calling immediately into the United States service one hundred thousand men from the States of Pennsylvania, Ohio, Maryland and Western Virginia; supplemented by a call on New York for twenty thousand more, all to serve for six months, unless sooner discharged. To this proclamation the various brigades of New York State National Guards respond with the greatest promptitude and alacrity. Special orders leap from numberless headquarters, while armories and arsenals are quickly alive with the first nervous movements of excitement.

Tuesday, 16th.—The whole city is moved with a common impulse. The rebel invasion; the startling call of the President; the alarming cry of Governor Curtin on New York for instant help; the energetic action of our State authorities; the thrice-tried patriotism of Massachusetts, reported as springing again to the rescue of Government with all her available militia force — all these conspire to animate every patriotic bosom with a fresh " On to Richmond " zeal. Militia men lose no time in reporting for duty, and volunteers bustle about to secure places in the ranks of their favorite regiments. A dozen regiments are under marching orders — a good deal of excitement and chagrin is caused by the rumored passage of the famous Massachusetts Sixth through the city. bound for the seat of war, beating New York a second time. The rumor proves to be unfounded. Orders are issued by Brigadier-General Jesse C. Smith to his Brigade, now comprising the 23d,

57th, 52d and 56th, to make instant preparations to leave for Harrisburg, Pennsylvania. for short service — three months or less, according to the emergency; there to report to Major-General Couch, commanding the Department of the Susquehanna.

Wednesday, 17th.—The gallant Seventh is the first in the field from the State, as is fitting. They are off at an early hour of the day, followed in the evening by the Eighth and Seventy-First. Martial enthusiasm pervades all classes, welling up from the several armories and overflowing the twin cities.

Thursday, 18th.—The Brooklyn Twenty-Third are ordered to assemble at their armory, corner of Fulton and Orange streets, at 7 o'clock, A. M., fully armed and equipped, and with two days' cooked rations in their haversacks, to march at 8 o'clock precisely. The gallant fellows are up with the larks : a hundred last things are done with nervous haste; father and brother give and receive the parting brave hand-grip; mother and sister and sweet-heart receive and give the last warm kiss; and with wet eyes, but in good heart, we set out for the rendezvous. There is remarkable promptitude in our departure. At the instant of 8 o'clock, — the advertised hour of starting, — the column

is moving down Fulton street toward the ferry.
The weather is auspicious — the sun kindly veiling his face as if in very sympathy with us as we struggle along under our unaccustomed burden. From the armory all the way down to the river it is a procession of Fairy-Land. The windows flutter with cambric; the streets are thronged with jostling crowds of people, hand-clapping and cheering the departing patriots; while up and down the curving street as far as you can see, the gleaming line of bayonets winds through the crowding masses — the men neatly uniformed and stepping steadily as one. Bosom friends dodge through the crowd to keep along near the dear one, now and then getting to his side to say some last word of counsel, or to receive commission to attend to some forgotten item of business, or say good-bye to some absent friend. As we make our first halt on the ferry-boat the exuberant vitality of the boys breaks out in song — every good fellow swearing tremendously, (but piously) to himself, from time to time, that he is going to give the rebels pandemonium, alternating the resolution with another equally fervid and sincere that he means to "drink" himself "stone-blind" on "hair-oil". What connection there is in this sandwich of resolutions may be

perhaps clear to the old campaigner. To passing vessels and spectators on either shore the scene must be inspiriting — a steamboat glittering with bayonets and packed with a grey-suited crowd plunging out from a hidden slip into the stream, and a mighty voice of song bursting from the mass and flowing far over the water. To us who are *magna pars* of the event, the moment is grand. Up Fulton street, New York, and down Broadway amid the usual crowds of those great thoroughfares, who waved us and cheered us generously on our patriotic way, and we are soon at the Battery where without halting we proceed on board the steamboat "John Potter" and stack arms. There is running to and fro of friends in pursuit of oranges and lemons — so cool and refreshing on the hot march — and a dozen little trifles with which haversacks are soon stuffed. One public-spirited individual in the crowd seizes the basket of an ancient orange-woman, making good his title in a very satisfactory way, and tosses the glowing fruit indiscriminately among the troops, who give him back their best "Bully Boy!" with a "Tiger!" added. Happy little incidents on every side serve to wile away a half hour, then the "all a-shore!" is sounded, the final good-bye spoken, the plank hauled in, and away we sail. A pleasant journey *via* Amboy and Camden brings us to Philadelphia at the close of the day. There we find a bountiful repast awaiting us at the Soldiers' Home Saloon, after partaking of which we make our way by a long and wearisome march to the Harrisburg Depot. At night-fall we are put aboard a train of freight and cattle cars rudely fitted up, a part of them at least, with rough pine boards for seats. The men of the Twenty-Third Regiment having, up to this period of their existence, missed somehow the disciplining advantages of "traveling in the steerage," or as emigrants or cattle, cannot be expected to appreciate at sight the luxury of the style of conveyance to which they are thus suddenly introduced. But we tumble aboard and dispose ourselves for a miserable night. A few of us are glum, and revolve horrible thoughts; but the majority soon come to regard the matter as such a stupendous swindle as to be positively ridiculous. They accordingly grow merry as the night waxes, and make up in song what they lack of sleep.

Friday, 19th.—The darkest night has its morrow. We reach Harrisburg thankfully a little after daybreak, and bid adieu, with many an ill-suppressed imprecation, to the ugly serpent that has borne us tormentingly from Philadelphia. Just sixty-four hours have elapsed since the orders were promulgated summoning the Brigade to arms. We are marched at once to Camp Curtin, some three miles out of town, and in the afternoon countermarched to town and thence across the Susquehanna to the Heights of Bridgeport — the latter being accomplished through a rain storm. As we enter the fort the Eighth and Seventy-First, N. Y. S. N. G., which had got a few hours' start of us, move out, taking the cars for Shippensburg on a reconnoisance.

II.

CAMP LIFE ON THE SUSQUEHANNA.

In hastening thus to the rescue of our suddenly imperiled government, we gave ourselves to that government without reserve, except that our term of service should not be extended beyond the period of the present exigency. Ourselves stirred with unbounded enthusiasm as we fell into line with other armed defenders of the Fatherland, we expected to find the inhabitants of the menaced States, and especially the citizens of Harrisburg, all on fire with the zeal of patriotism. We expected to see the people everywhere mustering, organizing, arming; and the clans pouring down from every quarter to the Border. At Harrisburg a camp had indeed been established as a rendezvous, but no organized Pennsylvania regiments had reported there for duty. The residents of the capital itself appeared listless. Hundreds of strong men in the prime of life loitered in the public thoroughfares, and gaped at our passing columns as indifferently as if we had come as conquerors, to take possession of the city, they cravenly submitting to the yoke. Fort Washington, which we were sent to garrison, situated on what is known as Bridgeport Heights, we found in an unfinished state. In the half-dug trenches were — whom, think'st, reader? Thousands of the adult men of Harrisburg, with the rough implements of work in their hands, patriotically toiling to put into a condition of defence this the citadel of their capital? Nothing of the sort. Panic-stricken by the reported approach of the enemy, the poltroons of the city had closed their houses and stores, offered their stocks of merchandize for sale at ruinous prices, and were thinking of nothing in their abject fear except how to escape with their worthless lives and their property. In vain their patriotic Governor, and the Commander of the Department of the Susquehanna — his military headquarters established there — sought to rally them to the defence of their capital. Hired laboring men were all we saw in the trenches! What a contrast to this the conduct of the Pittsburghers presents! They too had a city to defend — the city of their homes. The enemy threatened it, and they meant to defend it. Their shops were closed; their furnace and foundry fires, which like those watched by the Vestals had been burning from time immemorial, were put out; and the people poured from the city and covered the neighboring hills, armed with pick and shovel. "Fourteen thousand at work to-day on the defences," says the Pittsburg *Gazette* of the 18th June. Such a people stood in no need of bayonets from a neighboring State to protect them; while the apathy of the Harrisburghers only invited the inroads of an enterprising enemy.

And so the Twenty-Third was ordered into the trenches! This was so novel an experience to the men that they took to it pleasantly, and for two days did their work with a will. It must have been amusing, however, to an on-looker of muscle, in whose hands the pick or spade is a toy, to watch with what a brave vigor hands unused to toil seized and wielded the implements of the earth-heaver; and how after a dozen or two of strokes and the sweat began to drop, the blows of the pick grew daintier, and the spadefuls tossed aloft gradually and not slowly became spoonfuls rather. But we rallied one another and dashed the sweat away; and again the picks clove the stony masses damagingly, and the shovels rang, and the parapets grew with visible growth. Gangs of men relieved each other at short intervals; and in this way we digged through Saturday and Sunday.

On our arrival at the fort we found tents pitched ready to receive us, just vacated by the New York 8th, and 71st, before alluded to. But we were ordered to shift camp a day or two afterward and accordingly had the work of camp-making to do over. The site selected was a rather steep hillside, where the pitching of tents involves a good deal of digging. First, you must level off a rectangular plot some six feet by seven as a foundation for your structure. (This description refers to the "A" tent, ours being of that pattern.) Then you must set your tent-poles in such positions as that the tent, when pitched shall preserve nicely the rectilinearity of the street and its own equipoise. After that the canvas is stretched into proper position by means of pegs driven firmly into the ground on every side. Then follows carpentry work. Three or four joists, if you can procure them, are laid flat on the ground and half imbedded in the soft earth, and across these is fitted a board flooring. A pole is next adjusted close under the ridge-pole of the tent to accommodate a variety of furniture, whose shape or appendages suggest such disposition. And finally, a rack or framework is set up next the rear wall of the tent, for the support of the muskets of the mess.

Thus furnished, a tent has all the essential parts which belong to it in a well-ordered camp, according to the domiciliary fashions prevailing in the Twenty-Third Regiment. But beside these there are certain other constructions that seem to spring with the ease and grace of spontaneity from the hands of an ingenious and experienced contriver of a tent-home,—if so sacred a word may be used in so profane a connection. Not a little ingenuity is called into play in disposing advantageously about the tent the necessary personal paraphernalia of the soldier, not to mention the dozen little conveniences that incommode everybody, but which, nevertheless, silently accumulate by virtue of the volunteer's perpetual outreach after the shadow of his accustomed home comforts. Room must be found for four to six muskets, according to the number of the mess, and as many knapsacks, haversacks, belts, blankets, rubber-cloths, canteens, sets of dishes (!), boots or shoes, and a box to hold blacking and brushes, soap, candles, etc. Beside these, there is apt to be—unless the mess pass, as they ought to do, a prohibitory law on the subject—an assortment of towels, hand-

kerchiefs, stockings and other articles of apparel
which the owners thereof have lately washed, or
have gone through the motions of washing, and
have hung up overhead to dry, where they are forever flapping in your face when you stand upright
in the tent. The blankets and knapsacks are at night
used to eke out the appointments for sleep,—the
first to soften the floor to the bones of the sleepers,
the second to serve for pillows. These, especially
the former, are looked upon by the genuine soldier
as effeminate; while the greenhorn bitterly com-
plains of them as a very satire on helps to sleep.

There are nooks in a tent, as there are in every
builded house, that seem to be just the places for
some little oddities of contrivance or other. But
there is one appendage in particular which is quite
apt to possess the mind of the greenhorn. He is
early disgusted with the dirty, grovelling life of your
easy-going, shiftless, contented old campaigner, and
inwardly resolves to adopt a genteeler regimen.
So he builds him a cellar for the cool deposit of
wines, butter, milk, eggs, and whatever other delicacy his dainty stomach may require. In the tent
flooring he cuts a trap door admitting to the sacred
enclosure. You are reclining perhaps in your do-
micile opposite, dreamily coloring your meer-
schaum, and watching Mr. Greenhorn. As his work

developes itself to your comprehension you wrinkle your face with mischievous merriment, wondering whether he does not see, as you do, that there is a laugh to come in there by and bye. The day passes and time wags merrily on. A day or two afterward, at a certain "fall in for rations!" you notice in your enterprising neighbor an unusual nervous restlessness and a disposition, now for the first time shown, of winking slily at you without provocation, and chucking you in the ribs. You know at once that there is something in the wind, and suspect that the aforesaid laugh is to come in pretty soon. Instinctively connecting his conduct with that cellar which so much amused you, you are curious enough to follow up the thread he has unwittingly slipped into your fingers. Accordingly when he returns to his tent with provender in hand you watch him closely. He lifts the trap door and draws out a crock of butter, enough to last the mess a fortnight. With this unctuous gold of the dairy he overspreads his tough hard tack and shares his happiness with his messmates. You slily give the alarm to the street, and in a minute there is poking in at the tent door and overhanging the festive party a struggling crowd of hands, each bearing in its fingers a hard tack, or fragment thereof, clamorous to be buttered. You return to your tent roaring

with laughter, and subsequently observe that your
dismayed neighbour is spared the trouble of returning
the crock to the cellar! The same cruel
fate awaits a crock of milk which he was lucky
enough to get of the old woman under the hill, but
so impolitic as to expose in broad daylight on the
company parade. His wine—for it is evident there
is something of the sort in reserve,—he resolves—
so you infer,—to manage more astutely. Accordingly
in the sly of the evening, the flaps of his
tent closely drawn, though not so closely as to keep
out a mischievous eye, the stump of a tallow candle
shedding a forlorn, nebulous light on the assembled
mess, he draws forth a bottle of fine old sherry. It
is not long before sounds of merriment, of singing
and shouting and laughter, betoken an unusual
cause of excitement within that tent. There begins
to be a movement among outsiders, and you
proceed presently to make an investigation. You
peep in; another joins you; then another; and soon
there is a crowd. All make themselves at once
quite at home, sitting down on the edge of the
tent, on each other, on the ground, anywhere.
The master of the feast is by this time overflowing
with the milk—the wine rather—of human kindness.
He feels no dismay now at the sight of
his uninvited guests, but greets them with cordial

and good humored welcome, not noticing in his mellow mood, as you do, coolly surveying matters, that another of the aforesaid laughs will come in presently. His self-love all a-glow with satisfaction, he offers you a "glass of wine," (in a tin cup). You take the bottle also, and pass it around. He makes absurd speeches at which he laughs with boisterous glee, and at which you laugh too, and all laugh. He sings absurd medleys for which you improvise absurd choruses which make things go along as pleasantly as possible. Meanwhile the bottle is returned empty. He takes it, insists upon re-filling your "glass" from it, and tips it up over your cup. Then with a comical leer at you at the idea of attempting to pour wine from an empty bottle, he turns, dives into his cellar and fishes up another. You bid him go on with that capital song, offering to save him the trouble of unsealing and dispensing the jolly red wine. All grow rapidly merry, and so flows with a like looseness the song and the solace, till both are exhausted; and as the hour of "taps" approaches you bid your duped and fuddled host good night. The crowd follows suit, and soon the five small strokes of the drum find the company street deserted, lights extinguished, and each tent tenanted by its own for the night, though there still lingers in the air a suppressed murmur of drowsy song and laughter. (*Moral:*—A knowing campaigner never builds him a wine cellar.)

To our tent city we gave the name of Camp Couch in honor of our aforetime fellow-citizen of Brooklyn, the distinguished Major-General commanding the department. In acknowledging this honor the General remarked that he "was not unmindful of the great service rendered by our regiment and the troops of New York in so promptly responding to the call of our commanders to assist in repelling the threatened invasion of Pennsylvania." The life of duty we led there is well outlined in the following programme for each day, published in General Orders:—

"4.50 A.M. Drummer's call.

5.00 A.M. Reveille:—when roll will be called by the First Sergeant, (superintended by a commissioned officer,) on the company parade,—the troops parading without arms. Captains will report absentees without leave, to the commanding officer.

5.30 A. M. Police call :— when the quarters will be policed, as also the grounds immediately around them.

7.00 A. M. Breakfast call.

8.00 A. M. Guard mounting :— at this time the police party will parade without arms and police the grounds.

8.30 A. M. Surgeon's call: — when the sick will be paraded (?) by the First Sergeant and marched to the Surgeon's quarters to be examined (?).

9.00 A. M. Drill call:—for company drills.

12.00 M. Dinner call.

4.00 P. M. Drill call.

5.30 P. M. Assembly.

5.45 P. M. Evening parade, when the weather permits; at which time there will be by company an inspection of arms, cartridge boxes, and cap pouches. "Retreat" will beat off at every parade, and orders will be published.

9.00 P. M. Tattoo:—roll call without arms;— any special instructions to troops published.

9.30 P. M. Taps:—when all lights will be put out in quarters except the Guard House, the quarters of the Officer of the Day and Head-Quarters.

When the long-roll beats every one will repair without delay, armed and equipped, to his company parade ground.

All firing except by sentinels in enforcing orders and giving alarms is strictly prohibited. All loaded muskets will be kept at half-cock and great care taken in disposing of them and handling them. No troops will carry arms with fixed bayonets either in or out of quarters."

Our stay at Bridgeport Heights was so brief that the daily recurring camp duties had not time to crystallize into wearisome routine. Each day was enlivened by some novelty or amusing incident or other, which served alike to break the monotony of our work, and to hurry forward the hours with pleasing animation. Besides, the spot itself was pretty, and the views from it as beautiful as woods and water and mountains and far-spread blooming valleys, could well conspire to produce.

Toward the river the hill descends by a double slope, — the upper gentle, the lower abrupt. The camp was spread upon the former,— the company streets looking off toward Harrisburg and terminating at the brow of the bluff. The latter was covered with timber, but so thinly toward the top as not to intercept the view. Looking down from the crest of this bluff the eyes rest upon a ribbon of land one hundred feet below, dotted over with small white houses and little plots of garden, and divided lengthwise by a country road. Beyond is the river, in the midst of which lie four or five wooded islands. One of these stretches up and down for a mile or more, and is made picturesque by cultivated fields and a farm house nestled among trees. The river is moreover broken in the present stage of the water by innumerable shallows where tall grass grows. These green islets appear to be Meccas to the neighborhood cows; for you may see them daily in solemn file making pilgrimage thither by the fords. The opposite shore spreads out in a plain on which stands Harrisburg clustered about its looming capitol. The landscape up the river is bounded by the Blue Ridge, five miles off, which melts away behind the city in the far distance. Through these mountains the Susquehanna has broken its way, forming a gap whose abrupt sides finely relieve the monotony of the range. From the summit of the camping ground the view down the river is even more charming. There the eye wanders over an immense region warm with ripening wheat fields and white farm houses, and cool with hills, woods and water. In the distance the winding river, alternately hidden and revealed by jutting headlands and retreating intervales, loses its proper character and becomes to the eye a cluster of lakes embosomed in woods. Of these lakes you may count ten or a dozen.

In the first days of our tent life, before the hillside had become a nuisance, it was pleasant, of a warm forenoon, after the morning drill was over, to sit under the trees at the foot of the camp, and catch the cool breeze as it crept up the bluff. Here the news was read; here the rations were eaten and the

siesta enjoyed,— though stay-at-homes may think
the latter an absurdly superfluous luxury, taking
into consideration the quality of the former! Here
the letters from home — so welcome to the soldier
— were devoured again, and with his inverted plate
for a writing desk, roughly answered. Here some
dreamed reveries, and gazed across the river
anxiously homeward, remembering the advancing
columns of the enemy and the perils of our situation. Here we discussed the cupidity and pol-
troonery of the Harrisburgers, the ever-shifting
probabilities of the campaign, the loveliness of the
landscape, the demoralizing influences of camp life,
be it never so guarded, and the vivid contrasts of
home comforts and refinements with the coarseness and discomforts of our present lot.

It would be pleasant to rehearse the many
scenes and events which filled up our days in
camp:—the duties of the guard, alternately roasted
under the glaring sun of the parapet, and suffo-
cated in the crowded guard-tent; the varied em-
ployments of the police, — the scavengers and
involuntary retainers of the day,—now scrambling
in irregular file down the bluff carrying pails and
canteens for water, now bearing from the commissariat huge armfuls of bread, or boxes of hard
tack, or quarters of fresh beef, or sides of less appe-

tizing bacon, now "putting things to rights" in the street of the company, and called on all day long for multitudinous odd little jobs; the foraging parties dragnetting the country round for sheep, poultry, eggs, milk, and the like,—and this not to the owner's loss be it remembered; the morning wash in the Susquehanna; the evening swim; the drills and dress parades; the half-holiday in Harrisburg, whose baths and restaurants and shops, whose fair ladies, (where there were cherry-trees in the garden!), whose verandahs with easy chair and a Havana and quiet, made the place to us a soldiers' paradise; and this notwithstanding the mean spirit of the people made us despise them. Nor should mention be omitted of the benevolent visits of Harrisburg matrons to our hospital, bearing to the invalid sympathy with timely comforts.*

It would be pleasant to linger around the doors of the tents in the hush of a beautiful evening,

---

* And here it seems no more than common gratitude to mention a name, though to do so is to "break the custom" of this history. Through all those days and nights of terror there was one house in Harrisburg—and it is to be hoped many others, also—from which the starry banner was ever kept flying. The noble lady of this house solicited the privilege of receiving into her family any of our men who might be taken seriously ill. Her generous wish was complied with, and one of our number—how many others I know not—owed, doubtless, to her kind nursery, the blessed privilege of getting home to die in the bosom of his family. The regiments ought not soon to forget the name of Mrs. Bailey.

when, the work of the day ended, a sort of vesper service would be improvised, and melodies commemorative of love, home, patriotism and human freedom sung ; or a box, enticingly suggestive, just received from home, would be opened, and its contents of various dainties distributed with openhanded liberality to regale a score of comrades. It would be pleasant to recal, incident by incident, the evening meetings under the open sky for prayer, the affectionately pleading and encouraging words of our gentle chaplain, the hymn of trust and hope, the supplication of the volunteer whose lips were touched with tender remembrance of loved ones far away, into whose faces he might never look again. But important events await our narrative and we must hurry forward.

While we were thus quietly encamped, our gallant comrades of the Seventy-First and Eighth Regiments N. Y. S. N. G., whose places we had taken on our arrival at Bridgeport Heights, were having an active and arduous campaign at the front. On the evening of the 19th these two regiments under command of Colonel Varian, of the Eighth, proceeded to Shippensburg, "for the purpose," says Col. Varian in his report, quoting from the orders he had received, " of holding the enemy in check, should he advance; but under all circumstances to avoid an engagement; but if pressed too hard, to retire slowly and harass him as much as possible; the object being to give our forces at Harrisburg time to finish the fort and other defences, and be in readiness to receive the enemy should he advance to that point." On the 28th they arrived back in camp, having satisfactorily and most gallantly accomplished all they were sent to do. "It was," as General Couch remarked in a congratulatory order, "one of the most successful expeditions he had ever seen accomplished, according to the number engaged in it: viz., advancing fifty-two miles beyond all defences and support in case of an attack, and holding the enemy in check for a period of six days."*

Friday, 26th.—Commandants of regiments ordered to have their commands in immediate readiness to move or attack. Commandant of artillery

---

* The following thrilling incident is narrated by Col. Varian:— "Upon arriving within a mile of Chambersburg, I received intelligence that our cavalry pickets had been driven in, and the enemy's cavalry were about entering the town. I halted my command. * * * loaded the muskets, and started for the town. Marched down the principal street in column by companies * * * amid the enthusiastic plaudits of the whole population,—they looking upon us as their deliverers, and receiving us with a welcome that must be seen and felt to be properly appreciated, entertaining the entire command with such refreshments as could be hastily procured. * * * And amid the general congratulations the Stars and Stripes were run up the flagstaff amid the wildest enthusiasm."

in the Fort to see that his guns are in position, and that he has the requisite amount of ammunition.

Our camp, like every community, had its share of alarmists, who daily saw or heard of the enemy within five miles, ten miles, fifteen miles of us; at Carlisle, just beyond Carlisle, or wherever the thermometer of their fears placed him. Indeed the above orders, so closely following each other, had a decidedly threatening look. Still the opinion of those who had most faith in General Hooker, notwithstanding the tangled rumors of the hour, was that we should not see the enemy unless we went in pursuit of him; and to this pass we quickly came. It appears that information had been received at head-quarters, that the invaders had reached the vicinity of Carlisle, some eighteen miles west from Harrisburg, our small force having fallen back before them. They were said to have anywhere between five thousand and twenty thousand men, and to be advancing rapidly. These transpiring events, if true, were stirring enough, and gave a fine edge to an order on Friday for a reconnoissance by the whole regiment. We marched out of the fort with very uncertain feelings. The rain was falling, but we thought little of that: the roads were heavy — that troubled us more.

When the head of the column had reached a point some four miles or more out, we were halted. There were two parallel roads, a short distance apart, to be guarded. On these barricades were erected. Pickets being posted, the remainder of the regiment rested for the night in barns, sheds, or whatever offered shelter. Lively sensations must have coursed through the breasts of those who were now for the first time called to perform the duties of the night picket—a duty always trying, and particularly so now, in that we supposed we were in the near presence of a watchful and enterprising foe, who was advancing in force against us.

Saturday, 27th.—The night passed without excitement beyond what the imaginations of those on duty may have experienced. No rifle shot was heard; no skulking foe, suddenly detected, was caught trying to escape;—though many a wind-shaken bush, doubtless, was taken for a dodging rebel, and many a stump threateningly ordered to halt! Some four miles out, on the Harrisburg and Carlisle railroad is a little settlement called Shiremanstown which was the scene of an adventurous incident. There, on Saturday, a small picket force was stationed. It was an outpost, selected on account of its commanding a view of the Carlisle road for some distance. The village contained a church which supported a steeple; and in the top of that steeple three or four of our men were posted as sentinels, to keep a bright lookout for the enemy; and, the moment the latter showed themselves, to ring the church bell for an alarm, and then take to their heels! However illy this skedaddling programme may have suited the men, it is not to be doubted that they would have performed their part well—both the skedaddling and the ringing. Each, doubtless, looked sharply to be the first to catch sight of the expected cavalry troop, coming tearing up the road; and each stood ready on the instant to give the preconcerted signal, and then to pick their way down the uncertain passages of the steeple and trust their safety to the loyalty of their legs. The position was a trying one, and the brave fellows who performed the duty have in their memory at least one animating picture of patriotic service. No enemy appeared, and the skedaddle was spared. Different was the fortune of the pickets who relieved ours if we may believe what some of our men, who visited the place some days afterward, were informed by the villagers. During the night the enemy made their appearance, the bell was rung and the skedaddle enacted! Rebel troopers coming up were in hot rage against the innocent residents, charging them with sounding the alarm, seeming not to suspect that the pickets of the Yankee militia could have shown such audacious enterprise. After dark we returned to the fort, reaching it about midnight through rain and mud, wet, hungry and weary.

Sunday, 28th.—A day of animation in camp, and to the timid few one of excitement and alarm. The troops in the fort are drawn up in line of battle, and assigned positions at the breastworks, where arms are stacked. The now dangerous guard-duty on the parapets is performed with the usual alacrity and promptitude, some of us perhaps not realizing the near presence of the enemy. There is great activity on every hand to perfect the defences, and guard against sharpshooters. Squads of men are sent out to cut down trees and destroy whatever may afford cover to an enemy. A lady-resident sends up word that she does not wish to have the trees about her house cut down, as she intends to stay, and wants the trees to protect her against the shot. Our engineer, without arresting the destructive process, sends back his compliments and advises the unterrified female to remove herself and traps to the other side of the river as expeditiously as possible.

It is an animating sight to watch from the parapet all these various operations going on. The crackling of branches draws attention to yonder tree which comes tumbling to the ground with a crash—others follow rapidly and the axmen's blows resound on every side. On yonder knoll a company of mowers are rapidly leveling the tall wheat. Here inside the fort an artillery officer is drilling a squad in artillery firing: and there a gang of contrabands, now for the first time, very likely, receiving wages for their labor judging by the spirit they throw into their work, are putting the finishing touches on the ditch and parapet. Outside yonder a squad of men is tearing in pieces a twig hut which workmen have built for their tools. And so the final work of preparation goes on with great spirit, and is soon completed. There are still no signs of the approach of the enemy except what we observe about us in a sort of expectant air among the officers, and in the *qui vive* of the whole garrison. The skirmishers have all been driven in however, and we are liable at any moment to be startled by the roar of the enemy's artillery, opening an assault.

While affairs were thus culminating in the fort, an exciting spectacle was presented outside. For several days previously we had seen, whenever we went down to the river-side to bathe, or to draw water from the well, a stream of people with farm and household properties, coming in by the Carlisle and river roads, and pouring across the long bridge into Harrisburg. By day or night this living stream seemed never to cease. Men, women and children, white and black, some in carriages, some in wagons, some on horseback, some on foot, hurried along. Their horses and cattle they drove before them. A portion of household furniture— such evidently as could be hastily removed — went jolting along in heavy field wagons into which it had been hurriedly tumbled. Loads of hay and grain, of store goods, and of whatever property of house or field was thought to be in danger of appropriation or destruction by the rebels was taken with them. Some had come from beyond Mason and Dixon's line, as was evident from the color and style of their servants. Of the unmistakable genus "Contraband" there was a large assortment also. They came along in straggling companies, their personal goods and small stock of cabin wares usually tied up in bundles and slung upon a stick across the shoulder. In fact the whole valley was literally pouring itself out northward, and in wild confusion. If in that motley crowd of fugitives there was one brave heart worthy to enjoy the free institutions which the starry banner symbolizes, he must have hung his head in shame as he passed under the shadow of the fort whose protection he sought, where he himself should have been, one of ten thousand ready at command to be hurled against the invaders. Time enough had elapsed since the danger first threatened for the removal to a place of safety of the greater part of the property which the enemy most coveted, and the subsequent marshaling of the farmers for defensive battle. But relying on the hope of the enemy being turned back before he could reach them, they had consulted only the interests of the harvest, and had gone on "gathering into barns." Those were trying days, it is true, and much sympathy ought to be felt for the citizen taken thus at disadvantage; but the cry of alarm had been raised, the Governor had summoned the people to arms, the central government seemed helpless to defend Harrisburg except as it was defended indirectly by the army of the Potomac then covering Washington, and the only certain reliance for the safety of the valley was the hastily raised militia, chiefly from a neighboring State.

During that never-to-be-forgotten Sabbath day, so strangely "kept," there was no flurry among the garrison, judging by the men of the Twenty-Third, nor any fear shown at any time among those upon whose courage the fate of Harrisburg seemed likely to rest. While in that threatened city the chief authorities were staggering under the herculean work of organizing an unwilling or at least an indifferent people into a disciplined force capable of resistance, and of infusing into them somewhat of the patriotic zeal which shone so brightly in the conduct of their fellow-citizens of Pittsburg; while in that city there was feverish alarm on every hand, and families were ignominiously flying with their household gods, crowding the railway trains and the common highways in their eagerness to escape; while the State officers were sending off to Philadelphia the archives of the capital, and were themselves hastening or preparing to remove to the metropolis, which was to be the provisional capital on the fall of Harrisburg; while there existed on the opposite side of the Susquehanna these symptoms of alarm, there prevailed among our untried but trusted men, coupled with animated speculations concerning the enemy, the calmness of a summer evening. And this when it was evident to most that there was an enemy just outside our ramparts whose strength was supposed to be many times our own, and whose valor was renowned, waiting for the signal to be launched against us.

There may have been among the general officers

of the militia a feeling of anxiety. Indeed it would be strange were it otherwise. But this anxiety was doubtless due to the novelty of their position, together with their sense of the solemn responsibility which a commander bears in the hour of battle—a sense undulled in them by familiarity with scenes of carnage. But among the men there was the repose of confidence and courage. Whether hastily called to the breastworks and formed into line, expecting, it may be, to see the enemy drawn up on the distant hills; or dismissed with orders not to leave our company parade, and to lose not an instant in "falling in" at the first tap of the "Assembly," as the signal for regimental muster is called, or at the more ominous and alarming sound of the "Long-Roll;" whether retiring to our tents for the night, ordered to sleep on our arms; or awakened suddenly by the sharp "Halt! Who goes there?" of the passing sentinel; there seemed to cover the camp of the Twenty-Third— and the same was probably true of every other camp in that menaced stronghold — a mantle of repose such as they feel who fear no evil. Nevertheless had an assault been made with one-half the force, say, which carried the works of Winchester a few weeks previously, and with the same impetuous valor, there can hardly be two opinions as to the result. We should have resisted bravely and hurled back the enemy, green though we were; but a resolute persistence of assault by so superior a force would have compelled us to fly. For though our position was naturally strong its defences appeared to the uninitiated to be wretchedly inadequate. The number of mounted pieces was only thirteen, nearly all of which were three-inch rifles, carrying about a ten-pound bolt, manned, in part at least, by a militia company, tyros in the service of that arm, though as brave. patriotic and intelligent a set of men as the militia call had summoned to the field. Of the infantry only three or four regiments had been under fire, and these only in light skirmishes. Besides, the construction of the defensive works appeared to some of the unprofessional of us to be extremely faulty. The soil of the place is a slaty clay known geologically as *shale*. This being thrown up to form a breastwork constituted, as was thought by some of those whose duty it was to be to stand behind it and deliver their fire when the order came, a source of greater danger to them than rebel shot or shell. A ball striking the parapet near the top would have scattered a shower of stones into the faces of the men standing behind it, thus acting with almost as fatal effect as a shell bursting in the very midst of them. But it is to be presumed the fortifications were constructed on scientific principles by men specially trained for this business. At any rate, we were fortunately spared the experimental test of the theory.

Peculiarly impressive were the religious meettings we held, one in the forenoon and one at dusk, at which brave resolutions were reaffirmed with mutual plight, while the dear ones at home were remembered tearfully, and commended tenderly and trustingly to the Father's care. And it is pleasant to remember how, when the critical hour seemed to be at hand, our femininely sympathetic chaplain passed along the lines with a beaming countenance, bidding us rely on strength from above, and commending us with words of christian cheer to the divine protection.

Our greatest distress on that memorable Sabbath day was on account of our friends at home, stricken with fearful solicitude by reason of the dangers that impended over us, even tormented with skeleton rumors, as we learned, of "the enemy having engaged us;" of "our being cut to pieces;" of "crowds of wounded and dying troops being brought into Harrisburg from across the river." These lying reports we could not correct, since telegraphic and all other communication between camp and Harrisburg was at that time interdicted.

Had we known positively the intention of the enemy as since brought to light by the report of General Lee,* and that the famous old corps of Stonewall Jackson was but a few miles off, preparing to pounce upon us, we should not have felt so composed, nor lain down at night with so little anxiety about the morrow. As it was, many a lad wrapped himself in his blanket that night for a little uncertain slumber, expecting surely to be awakened by the "Long-Roll," and to be led forth to battle. But we slept tranquilly till the morning muster-call broke our dreams. The double force of sentinels that kept watch all night saw from the walls nothing more alarming than branches of trees or bushes nodding in the wind; though there is no witness to testify how often a stump or rock

---

* "Preparations were now made to advance upon Harrisburg; but on the night of the 29th, information was received from a scout that the Feleral army, having crossed the Potomac, was advancing northward, and that the head of the column had reached South Mountain. As our communications with the Potomac were thus menaced, it was resolved to prevent his further progress in that direction by concentrating our army on the east side of the mountains. Accordingly, Longstreet and Hill were directed to proceed from Chambersburg to Gettysburg, to which point Gen. Ewell was also instructed to march from Carlisle."—*Extract from Gen. R. E. Lee's Report of the Battle of Gettysburg.*

was challenged by them in their sleepless scrutiny of every suspicious thing around them.

Monday, 29th.—It was bruited about camp that the Twenty-Third would be called on to furnish a detail of men to go out as scouts, and many a breast fluttered with anxious debate upon the subject. Without, was danger and honor; within, security and shame. Who had the courage to go out to the very advance, taking his life in his hand, with no more than musket range between himself and the enemy? We had already been drawn up in line of battle, solemnly awaiting the enemy who was expected to open fire on us at any moment, and there had been no flinching. But then we had the moral support of numbers to keep up our courage. The whole regiment stood shoulder to shoulder and each man felt the safer for having his comrades all about him. But to go out from the presence of these comrades, to march out of the carefully guarded fort, where all were friends and defenders together, into the open country which the imagination filled with enemies; to take position alone in some distant covert perhaps, warily lying in wait like a wild Indian for the equally wary foe, when the pushing aside of a twig or the crumpling of leaves beneath the feet might betray you to your instant death; and so to watch for hours together whether by day or by night, in storm or in shine — this was something to try of what stuff we were made.

We were ordered up in line early in the day, and a call made for volunteers. Instantly five times the number needed stepped forward eager competitors for the post of danger. The squad was at once formed, and in company with similar detachments from the Eighth and Fifty-Sixth N.Y.S.N.G., marched out of the fort amid a tempest of cheers. When we saw that our brave comrades were really gone we turned back with heavy hearts, for it seemed to our imaginations that as their object was to spy out the enemy, they would not fail to find him, and that then there would be unavoidably an action, which meant death to some. We conjectured sadly which one of these brave fellows it might be upon whose living face we had looked for the last time; who, the first of us all, should have bound about his brows the laurel wreath of glory. At nightfall the Seventy-First returned to the fort from the front.

Tuesday, 30th. — During the forenoon did little else than hold ourselves in readiness, keeping a bright lookout for the enemy; till at length we began to think — many of us with a speck of disappointment mingled with a sort of settled indifference—that we should lose the chance of giving him a taste of our quality. After noon we were ordered to shift camp. This augured serious work, inasmuch as the object of the movement was to contract the camp limits, and thus make room for more troops within the fort. After the order was issued directing us to prepare for removal it was curious to note what a change a few minutes produced in the appearance of the company streets. The first step was to clear tents. Before each door arms were stacked, and on a blanket spread on the ground were rapidly piled knapsacks, haversacks, blankets, boots and shoes, tin-ware, rough boxes, shelving, and an indescribable variety of loose matter; altogether an astonishing mass of tent furniture, considering that these canvas houses, some five feet by six in dimensions, accommodated—if so satirical a remark be allowed in sober history—four to six persons besides, according to luck and court favor. Next followed the order to strike tents. In a twinkling the white walls collapsed, and the sun glared down upon a field flat and waste. Each mess, directly on having their new site assigned them, went to work like beavers to rehabilitate their domicils, but it was dark before the new village was fairly settled. There remained, besides, for the morrow many supplementary items of work, among which was the building of company kitchens. Where the ground is level no preparation of it is needed for this purpose; but on a steep slope a good deal of digging is necessary. Indeed where there is any considerable slope whatever, it is better to level the ground. Labor in constructions for the benefit of your culinary corps is most judiciously invested. A broad and level plat with convenient arrangements for boiling the pot and preparing the rations, the whole covered with a screen of some sort from the sun and the weather, will give you better coffee, better soup, better everything—not to speak of the occasional substitution of a bake or a roast in place of the inevitable boil—than if you have failed to provide for the comfort of your cooks. All this can be done easily where there are so many interested hands to help. An enterprising head to manage and direct operations is the common want. Possessing that a company is pretty sure to have a successful culinary department ; and just this makes all the difference between excellent and execrable rations. The commissary supplies of the army, judging by the experience of the Twenty-Third, are abundant and good: better, it is believed, than the average fare of American farmers, except in the matter of fresh vegetables; but bad cooking spoils the best rations.

To construct a plat on a steep slope for the kitchen: lay out a square of liberal dimensions — eight feet on a side should be a minimum perhaps. Along the lower side and half-way up the adjacent sides firmly drive stiff stakes, sixteen or eighteen inches apart, reaching a little above the destined level of the plat, and pile bushes or twigs against them on the inner side, interweaving them as much as possible, and making a matted wall. Then with pick and spade dig down along the upper side of the square, and half-way along the adjacent sides, tossing the earth against the twig wall, and packing it well down, till you have a level to suit you. There will be subsequently a gradual subsidence of the loose earth to some extent, against which you must provide. The centre of course must be the highest part in order to shed rain. If the soil be clayey, you will have a sticky mud with every fall of rain unless you put on a covering of gravel, slate, or the like. On one side steps should be dug out leading down from the table where rations are dispensed. Stakes should be driven at the extremities of the steps so as to hold firmly a stiff limb of a tree or a stick laid against them and along the edge of the step. Without this precaution your steps will not last longer than a day or two. If boards for a shed are not to be had, a bower can be constructed of branches of trees, such as any old soldier knows how to build.

Wednesday, July 1st. — Picket force returned without loss; but they had met the enemy, as the following report of the Officer Commanding will show :—

"Fort Washington, Harrisburg, Pa. }
July 1st, 1863. }

COLONEL WM. EVERDELL, Jr.,
    Commanding 23rd Reg. N. G. S. N. Y.
  COLONEL :—

    I have the honor to report that in compliance with General Orders No.———of June 29th, from Gen. Knipe, commanding Second Brigade of First Division of the Army of the Department of the Susquehanna, I assumed command of a detachment composed of three companies, viz.: one from the 8th, one from the 23rd, and one from the 56th regiments of the N. G. S. N. Y.— in all about 150 men — for picket duty at Oyster Point Station ; this being the advance post, and about three miles to the front and west of Harrisburg. Before arriving at the front I heard heavy cannonading at intervals of from five to ten minutes. Fearing a sudden attack, and not knowing the strength or intention of the enemy, I hastened without loss of time to establish my pickets, detaching for that purpose a portion of company——, 8th regiment, commencing from the Carlisle turnpike in a direction due north across the fields and beyond the railroad; and establishing in a like manner a portion of the 23rd regiment from the Carlisle road due south, under command of Lieut.————of company—— 23rd; thus guarding the main roads and entrances to the city of Harrisburg.

While thus engaged in throwing out my sentries the firing from the enemy increased, and became more rapid, evidently with the intention of shelling us from our position. I therefore, as soon as practicable, deployed the companies of the 8th and 23rd regiments as skirmishers, keeping the remaining company as a reserve.

To gain a better position, and to obtain a clearer view of the enemy's location, I advanced over a cornfield to a small wood situated on more elevated ground. But on entering this wood we were exposed to a constant fire of shot and shell from the rebel batteries. Fortunately none of our men were disabled or wounded. The skirmishers advanced about the distance of a mile, keeping up a steady fire. At 4 P. M., firing gradually ceased, and scouts returned reporting the enemy having fallen back.

Late in the evening I was informed that small groups of rebels had been seen in the immediate vicinity; and to guard as much as possible against being surprised, I sent out a squad of the reserves of the 56th regiment as videttes, doubled the guards, and carefully reconnoitered to the front, and north and south of the Carlisle and Chambersburg road, but failed to discover any enemy in our vicinity, until 3 A.M. of Tuesday, the 30th, when two of their scouts were seen endeavoring to get inside our lines. Our pickets fired upon them and wounded one through the knee, and took him prisoner; the other escaped. The prisoner stated that he and his companion belonged to General Jenkins' Brigade of Virginia troops, and that they were bearers of despatches to that rebel general. At 9 A. M., I received a communication from Gen. Knipe ordering me to return with my command to Fort Washington.

I cannot speak in too high praise of both officers and men * * * * for their willingness and alacrity to execute every order issued, for their watchfulness and vigilance, and for their determination displayed while momentarily expecting to be attacked by the enemy. * * * * *

Yours respectfully,

JOHN A. ELWELL,

Lt.-Col. 23rd Reg. N. G. S. N. Y. Com. Detachment.

III.

FORWARD !

We had just got settled in our new quarters when, on the afternoon of Wednesday 1st of July, came marching orders. The enemy was retiring and we were to give chase. We were ordered to provide ourselves with two days' cooked rations and to move completely equipped, with packed knapsacks, blankets, and all the paraphernalia of a marching column. This included a square of canvas, two of which buttoned together, constitutes what is called a shelter-tent, for the accommodation of two men. This pointed plainly enough to a vigorous campaign, and every man was pleased with the prospect. It was toward evening when we left the fort, taking the Carlisle road. Though the day was warm we kept up a brave spirit for some two or three miles, singing and shouting, stimulated by the exciting expectation of meeting the enemy face to face, and animated by the beauty of the country through which we were passing. But after an hour or so our heavy burdens, the still hot sun, and the roughly macadamised road began to tell on us. Some becoming exhausted were relieved of a part of their load by officers, or by comrades who were stronger; field and staff officers in several instances gave up their horses to the o'erwearied ones; while other riders piled up knapsacks and blankets before them and behind them till they were almost sandwiched out of sight. One fellow was noticed who had been so lucky as to pick up a small hand-cart on which he had packed his luggage, and had induced, by means of an emollient of greenbacks, a small boy to drag it along. In such ways as this, and by rendering each one to his neighbor a little timely help now and then, we managed to reach Trindle Spring Creek, a small stream which crosses the road about seven miles out from Fort Washington; though when we think of the weight we bore, of the warm afternoon, and of our being totally unused to such hardships, it is a little remarkable that we got through so well. The following tabular statement exhibits the actual avoirdupois weight of our equipments — a fair average being taken, some being more and some less than the estimate.

	lb.	oz.
Musket,	10	8
Belt, etc.,	1	10
Forty rounds ball cartridges,	3	6
Knapsack, packed,	9	0
Haversack, containing two days' rations, with a few trifling extras,	2	0
Woolen Blanket,	5	8
Rubber do.	2	8
Canteen, half-filled,	2	8
Overcoat,	5	0
A half shelter-tent,	2	0
Total,	44 lbs.	

This is about the weight of a healthy boy, eight years old. Some carried even more than this, viz.— an extra pair of heavy government shoes, together with an assortment of tins, such as cup, plate, teapot, etc.

We were halted in a clover field a little after ten o'clock. The night was dark, the sky being overcast; and here we had our first bivouac. No sooner had we reached the spot than we saw what convinced us that we had entered in good earnest upon the business for which we professed to have left our homes; for far away to the front rose the heavy boom of artillery firing, and a bright light reflected from the clouds indicated that a conflagration was raging in the same vicinity, probably at Carlisle. This proved to be a demonstration of the rebel General Fitz Hugh Lee against the small force of militia under General W. F. Smith then holding Carlisle. The former it appears was escorting a train which was on its way toward Chambersburg, and fearing an attack from General Smith made a show of taking the offensive and demanded a surrender of the place. This was refused; whereupon the rebel officer contented himself with shelling the town, which resulted principally in the burning of the government cavalry barracks situated there. At length having by his audacity gained security for the train he withdrew. In recognition of the service rendered to Carlisle by General Smith on this occasion of alarm, some ladies of the place have since presented to him the compliment of a silver urn :— the only instance, by the way, which the citizens or government of Pennsylvania is known to have furnished of their appreciation of the service they received at the hands of the New York Militia.

On coming to a halt in the field of our bivouac, our officers were considerate enough to spend but little time in getting us into line and stacking arms. Straps were unbuckled and luggage tumbled, a dead weight, to the ground in less time than it takes to tell it. We spread our rubber blankets upon the wet grass, and drawing on our overcoats dropped down to rest, each man behind his musket. Some of the less weary went in search of water to drink, and some had the wisdom to bathe their hot, overworked feet in the neighbouring brook.

It was a new experience to most of us — this lying down with the clouds for our coverlid, and serenaded with the music of distant battle. Though we did not wrap ourselves up sentimentally in the dear old flag, it seemed as if the God of battles looked down from on high upon our shelterless condition, and folded us in his own more glorious banner of clouds. If our anxious mothers could have seen us at that moment lying down to sleep without protection from the night air and the rain which threatened, they would have most piteously bewailed our lot. Many of us expected that the morning would find us coughing, sneezing and wheezing, or moping about feverish on account of broken sleep, if not pinned to the ground by the sharp needles of rheumatism. But notwithstanding the strange sounds which filled our ears and our imaginations, we hardly had time, after stretching ourselves upon the ground, to review our situation before sleep caught us: and we slept gloriously well. Not a man of us, it is probable, who made a prudent use of blanket and overcoat, but rose next morning refreshed.

Now that the stirring events of those days are history it may be interesting to notice as we go along the rapid evolution of the drama of Gettysburg, which we, so lately menaced in our stronghold at Fort Washington, little dreamed was being consummated with such tremendous suddenness. It was so lately as the Sunday just passed that we were kept under arms all day expecting an assault from Ewell, who was known to be threatening Harrisburg with the greatest part of his corps. On Monday the reconnoissance had developed the presence of the enemy still investing our position. But on the night of Monday, 29th, Lee first learned with surprise of the dangerous proximity of Gen. Hooker, threatening his communications, and resolved to concentrate his now somewhat scattered army eastward of the South Mountains. Accordingly Ewell must have moved off from our front the same night, or early on Tuesday morning, since he re-appears upon the scene on Wednesday afternoon at Gettysburg, where he arrived between one and two o'clock, P. M.—just in time to check, with the aid of other reinforcements, the advance of General Reynolds and to drive him back with heavy loss. These reinforcements must all have made forced marches and they could have been in no condition to follow up the advantage gained. Lee was doubtless well content to have turned back, with his fatigued battalions, the rising tide of victory, and *nolens volens*, left General Howard, who succeeded to the command of the field on the fall of the lamented Reynolds, at liberty to establish himself unmolested on the now famous cemetery heights. It is interesting and instructive to notice further, that this corps of Ewell, whose reported withdrawal from the investment of Fort Washington was apparently the signal for our advance, reached Gettysburg, and was there instrumental in snatching victory from the jaws of defeat, absolutely before our movement began!

Thursday, July 2d.—At 3 A. M., we are aroused from sleep by a whispered summons to get ready to move at once without making the least noise! This looks like work. The reflection of the fire in front has disappeared, the cannonading is hushed, and all is still. What does it mean? A report comes flying through the field that the enemy have driven back our advance and that these are falling back upon our lines.

We waited under arms, looking as we stood there under the star-light drawn up over the whole field, like a spectral host. Was there a rebel ambuscade over yonder in the woods, watching for us to take up our unsuspecting march toward Carlisle in order to swoop down upon us unawares? A cowardly suggestion, but still one which occurred very naturally to raw troops thrust in this way into what, for aught they knew to the contrary. was the very front of danger. This was the first feeling; but soon we grew calmer and remembered that even if our advance had been compelled to fall back, they were still between us and the enemy; and that moreover if they had met with disaster, there would be fugitives enough very soon to tell the story.

We waited impatiently for orders to march; and waited, and waited, till at length dawn began to flush; and by and bye, when it was quite day, the column moved.

"The King of France, with twenty thousand men,
Marched up the hill and then—marched down again."

Back toward Harrisburg—one mile—two miles —three miles nearly : and there by the roadside we halted. Was the enemy in pursuit? Were we falling back to Harrisburg? Or what was the matter? Whether the halt was for five minutes or for all day every one was in blissful ignorance, including, very likely, our commanding officer himself, Brigadier-General Knipe.

We were in a tributary vale of the renowned Cumberland Valley, a beautiful farming country. Farm houses lay scattered along the road, almost within hallooing neighborhood of one another. Although the order was, on leaving the fort, that each man should provide himself with two days' cooked rations, yet some, in the hurry and excitement of departure, had been careless about it; while others had used their supply improvidently. Thus it happened that on this the very first morning after setting out, there were not a few hungry stomachs that had to trust to luck for their needful provender. Beside this there was a prejudice with many against "hard tack" and cold meat with spring water to wash them down; particularly when brought into competition with the possible supplies of a prosperous farmer's garden, cellar and field. It was not strange therefore, that there were eyes which rested greedily on every house we passed, nor that some of the men should improve the earliest moment when we came to a halt, to run for a call upon the nearest housewife.

Five minutes—ten minutes—half an hour—an hour; and still no move. It is evident the halt is more than a rest. Shelter-tents and rubber-cloths begin to appear along the fences, spread for a screen from the sun. Every near tree has its crowd of loungers underneath. At first it was only by the road side, but now the adjoining fields too must furnish their contribution of shade. Further off yonder a company of fellows are mixing promiscuously and socially among a herd of cows; in fact there is amateur milking going on, it is evident. Do you see that farm house three-fourths of a mile over yonder, glancing white among thickly clustering trees? and that string of lads along the fence down there, on their way toward it? They are bound thither, doubtless, in search of a comfortable breakfast. But they are not good soldiers to venture so far now. If the column should be ordered forward again before they return, they will be in trouble unless their officers fail to do their duty in the matter.

Another hour passes — it is ten o'clock — it is eleven o'clock — it is noon. By this time every man in the brigade has taken thought doubtless how to dispose of himself pleasantly or at least comfortably for the rest of the day. All are indifferent as to marching — everything about us having apparently come to a dead stand-still. The most absurd rumors have been flying about all the forenoon, the members of the Twenty-Third having nothing to do in their yawning idleness but to toss them back and forth like shuttlecocks. Among other luminous reports — the more alarming the more likely to be believed — is one that the rebels have struck in upon our line of communication by the flank and taken Fort Washington, ensuring the capture of the whole brigade. This ridiculous story finds credence in some coward bosoms, the wish being father to the thought; since capture means parole, and parole means home perhaps. Some one proposes to send out a party to gather up all the rumors that come floating in like drift wood and have them burned. It is needless to say that the proposition is handsomely received, but there appears to be practical obstacles in the way of carrying it out.

Some venturesome and enterprising foragers bring in word of a beautiful river one-third of a mile off; and as we have no orders against rambling, and as the provost guard is withdrawn, one squad after another breaks away, till there is hardly a corporal's guard left in charge of the arms. A few turns down a narrow little-traveled road edged with shade trees, bring us suddenly full upon a charming stream of water. It is a hundred or a hundred and fifty yards wide, swiftly flowing, and heavily wooded on the opposite side. On the hither bank it is bordered by a single row of gigantic oaks and willows, four to six feet through, standing within four to eight feet of the water, and almost on a level with it. Beneath these magnificent trees runs a country road leading to farm houses, suspected not seen, along the river. This stream rejoices in the euphonious name, as one of the residents there tried in vain to inform some of us, of the Conedoguinet.

Let us go close to the water. How charming! The grass grows heavy and green from the roadside under the dense shade of the oaks and willows to the very lips of the water; and the ground under our feet is so level and smooth that we have as perfect a walk as the Central Park can offer; and this is all the work of Nature. How clear the water is! We can see everything on the bottom with perfect distinctness. Rich green water plants bend their limbs gracefully to the force of the current. Old dead sticks lie stiff and stark, that once were living branches swaying and singing above their present burial places, not dreaming of death and decay, so beautiful were they. Great rocks heave their brown backs up to the very top of the water. Beds of gravel still and clear, glisten in the depths. Here the cool shade, there the warm sunshine. Here the smooth water, there the troubled current.

The temptation is great; dive in we must. The water, how cool it is and refreshing! But so shallow that in attempting to swim there is danger of abrading the knees against the bottom. We wash, we splash about with rollicking freedom, we lie down flat letting the water cover us and lift us again buoyant on its bosom, and bear us on with its current. What an infinite charm resides in the water about us! Beautiful the great trees under whose shade we lie. Beautiful the grassy bank — but lo! a small heap of dirty clothes on the greensward! We turn away with disgust and laughter. Insignia of glory! — a shilling's worth to the rag-picker. What a contrast they present to the loveliness of the common things around us!

Yonder other wanderers are having a more various enjoyment. They have fished out of the mud an old dug-out, leaky and every way disabled. But by dint of skillful engineering they have got her afloat and are pulling and paddling about, as happy, as free from care, and to complete the picture, as naked as any South Sea Islander in his merriest aquatic mood. Hither and thither, up and down, they float at their own sweet wills, having no orders from superior officers to obey. And this is part of a column supposed to be watching a vigilant and powerful enemy! What if the assembly should beat suddenly now ! There would be a pretty scampering truly.

Crawling reluctantly ashore again, we transform ourselves into United States soldiers, and trudge along the road by the river bank for a further reconnoissance. Others are going the same way; some are returning. We come to a farm house presently. A crowd is there ; among them a bevy of girls — healthy-looking, fair-skinned daughters of Pennsylvania farmers. They have been baking all day for the soldiers who never ceased coming, the stream increasing rather as the day advanced ; and as they must stop sometime, they have concluded to stop before they reach the bottom of the flour barrel. So we get nothing. They tell us there is a house on the other side of the river; and at the foot of the lane just down yonder we may find a boat to take us across. The boat is found, the ferry accomplished, the house reached, and there behold another crowd! It would be interesting to know what farm house for miles around the central halting place was unvisited on that day by some representative of the New York or Brooklyn militia. We find our comrades seated decently at table, positively eating with knives and forks, and drinking tea whitened with real cream! The turn of our crowd came soon. Fresh bread and butter, ham, sweetmeats, pickles, tea, and all without stint; and besides, clean white dishes to eat off! It seemed ridiculous; nevertheless, war or no war, enemy or no enemy, there was the staring fact! The thrifty housewife seemed disposed to be sociable while we were regaling ourselves, but not knowing how to go about it, was silent. Thus the onus fell upon us. So we began;—the crops, the weather, the soil, the neighbors, the invasion, the Great City. We had to ransack our heads for topics, each being quickly exhausted. We ate all our sharp appetites asked for; sharp they were, for it was now the middle of the afternoon, and we had been up since 3 o'clock A. M. Rising to go we offered money but the patriotic lady refused to look at it,— we were welcome to all she could do for us. So we addressed ourselves to the small fry of the family, and distributed little souvenirs among them. In this way all were made happier; and with a feeling of immense satisfaction we saluted our hospitable host adieu and made our way back without further delay to the regiment. The column was already moving,— their faces still turned toward Harrisburg. Accordingly we climbed under our fifty pounds of lumber again, and plunged along after with renewed vigor.

This absolute freedom of the country which appears to have been at the disposal of all, and indulged to such an extraordinary degree, may seem to cast a grave reflection either upon the discipline of the division or upon the efficiency of regimental officers. But it is plain that no blame justly attaches to either. For, the halt was made as a simple rest; and when, as the minutes multiplied, a provost guard was at length set, the men had already begun to straggle off little distances by ones, twos, and threes, to get better shade, or to fill canteens, or to seek better provender; and so the precaution came too late. Besides we had not yet established disciplinary habits as a moving column; and in the absence of all instructions or cautions on the subject from headquarters,* no regimental officer, how-

---

* On the next day Major-General Couch wrote the following order upon this important subject, which, strangely enough, was first promulgated, at least to the Twenty-Third, while we were lying at Waynesboro; indeed it was not published to the 52d until July 16th. This fact is a striking evidence of the vigor of the campaign on which we were entering.

Head-Quarters Department of the Susquehanna,
Harrisburg, July 3d, 1864.

GENERAL ORDERS No. 5.

The General commanding calls the attention of all the officers and soldiers in this Department to the vice of pillaging, which as yet exists only to a small extent. He trusts that all will unite in frown-

over intelligent, and however familiar theoretically with his duties, could be expected, if devoid of experience in active service, to foresee the exigincies of such an unusual occasion. The day in all its aspects was a surprise and an enigma to officers and men alike.

The column continued its retrograde movement and about sunset turned down a road that crosses the Conedoguinet at a place called Orr's Bridge, not far from a mile distant from the spot where we had lain all day; and on the hither bank of the river stacked arms for the night. It was a pretty place for a bivouac. The river, a hundred yards or more in breadth, here makes a sweep forming

---

ing upon the disgraceful practice, and in a determination to put an entire stop to it.

All military organizations of whatever extent, whether Army, Corps, Regiment, or Company, must remember that in order to gain for themselves a good reputation, it is essential that they preserve their record free from such stains.

Commanding officers will be held strictly accountable that private property is sedulously respected by every officer and man under them. They will also see that there is no straggling permitted on the march, or from the camps. If soldiers or officers fail in their duties, they should be at once arrested and reported to these Headquarters; and besides the military punishments provided, their names, with the number and designation of the regiment to which they belong, shall be furnished as a further disgrace, to the Adjutant-General of the State to which they belong.

By command of
MAJOR GENERAL D. N. COUCH.
JOHN S. SCHULTZE, Ass't-Adj't-Gen'l.

an arc of water, one third of a mile long, which flows placidly. The opposite shore, forming the inner curve of the arc, is tame, being covered for the most part with a straggling growth of timber; but on this side the river is flanked by a ridge along the top of which runs the Harrisburg and Carlisle pike. In the near distance, now lengthened by the deepening twilight, this ridge melts off into rolling hills, embrowned with ripe standing grain; while where the Twenty-Third made their bivouac it rises rough and precipitous, and is thickly wooded. All along the water's edge lies a narrow belt of lawn, thirty to forty feet wide, beautifully green and level, on which the brigade was halted. About midway of the arc of water, the stream is spanned by a bridge. As the darkness crept on, the picture presented from our bivouac was in the highest degree charming, and might be supposed to realize some sylvan poet's dream.

> "No bird-song floated down the hill,
> The tangled bank below was still.
>
> No rustle from the birchen stem,
> No ripple from the waters hem.
>
> The dusk of twlight round us grew,
> We felt the falling of the dew."

The lawn on which we sat down was in such harmony with the smooth water on one side, and in such contrast with the unsightly rocks on the other that one might be led to wonder whether some dreamer of old did not plant the spot for his evening walk and musing; nor was it strange that Fancy should bear us on her wings far back to the Golden Age of Story, and that we should dream of wood nymphs and water sprites, and the clime of Arcady.

Looking up stream the centre of the picture was occupied by the bridge, one hundred and fifty yards distant, with woods at either end. In the left foreground lay massed by foreshortening the long lines of stacked arms, with crowds of figures, some moving but most of them at rest. In the distance, under the bridge, this line bent gracefully around to the right of the picture. Half a hundred fires were blazing along the edge of the water, growing brighter every minute as the darkness thickened. Directly over the bridge hung the planet Venus, now moving in that part of her orbit where she shines with the greatest splendor. There were no clouds, the wind had fallen, and the air was delightfully cool. Supper being over we had sat down in companies upon the grassy bank to smoke and enjoy the incomparable scene. Every present influence tended to make us forget the enemy, and to call to mind only associations of the beautiful. Under such inspirations it was impossible to resist the impulse to sing. It was a thing of unsophisticated nature. Music came to our lips as if it were an instinct, as if it were the very condition of our being, just as if we had been birds. It will be difficult for any one not of that company to realize with what tender, touching pathos the simplest home melodies melted over those waters, though the words and airs might be trite and even trivial.

Some one started Morris' popular song of "Annie of the Vale":—

> " The young stars are glowing,
> Their clear light bestowing!
> Their radiance fills the calm, clear summer night!
> Come forth like a fairy,
> So blithesome and airy,
> And ramble in their soft mystic light!"

The chorus, by spontaneous impulse, welled out tenderly yet with grand effect :—

> " Come, come, come, Love, come!
> Come, ere the night-torches pale!
> Oh! come in thy beauty,
> Thou marvel of duty,
> Dear Annie, dear Annie of the Vale!"

Then all was hushed to listen to the melody again : —

> "The world we inherit
> Is charmed by thy spirit,
> As radiant as the mild, warm summer ray!
> The watch dog is snarling,
> For fear, Annie darling,
> His beautiful young friend I'd steal away!"

And the chorus broke in as before. A pause — and like a variation in the song of the nightingale, rose the pathetic air of the "Poor Old Slave"; —

> "'Tis just one year ago to-day
> That I remember well,
> I sat down by poor Nelly's side,
> A story she did tell;
> 'Twas about a poor unhappy slave
> That lived for many a year,
> But now he's dead and in his grave,
> No master does he fear."

All joining with subdued voices gave the chorus: —

> "The poor old slave has gone to rest,
> We know that he is free;
> Disturb him not, but let him rest
> 'Way down in Tennessee."

There were several favorite melodies which we had often sung in camp, when, as on a pleasant Sunday evening, we were met together in little knots, to mingle our emotions in plaintive song, thinking of dear friends at home. One of these was a simple ballad describing the following incident — one of the most touching of the war. A youthful soldier from the state of Maine died in New Orleans, with none but strangers—as has been the lot of many—to watch over him in his dying hours, or to perform the sad rites of burial. When the funeral service was over, and the coffin was about to be closed, an elderly lady present approached the remains, saying: "Let me kiss him for his mother."

> "Let me kiss him for his mother,
>   Let me kiss his dear youthful brow;
> I will love him for his mother,
>   And seek her blessing now.
> Kind friends have sooth'd his pillow,
>   Have watched his ev'ry care:
> Beneath the weeping willow,
>   Oh! lay him gently there.
>
> CHORUS: Sleep, dearest, sleep;
>   I love you as a brother;
>   Kind friends around you weep,
>   I've kissed you for your mother."

The words and melody harmonised with our feelings and lent them a deeper tone as our united voices floated out upon the soft, still evening air.

With songs of pathos, of love, and of home we mingled strong patriotic airs. But it was curious to observe how by a common instinct ev'rything like coarseness and drollery was avoided. The absurd rollicking songs, most popular on the march, were now scarcely hinted at. And in this way an hour passed into oblivion as softly as if we had been asleep dreaming of home which then was heaven, or near it. The bridge had become shadowy in the gathered darkness, the curve line of the bivouac was invisible except as it was dotted out by the blazing fires, the water gleamed with the dancing images of flame, and overhead thousands of stars had come out to be witness of our flow of soul. And now as the spirit of stillness was creeping over the enchanted valley, we spread our rubber blankets under the trees or the open sky, drew on our overcoats, and lay down to sleep.

Looking back over the events of that day of waiting, and our rose-colored bivouac in that lovely valley of the Conedoguinet, it is curious and instructive to observe how pretty a trap we had walked into unconsciously. It is suspected that the commander selected this spot for our bivouac from its cage-like character, being prompted thereto by the provoking experience of the day. However that may be, it is plain that had the enemy been as near us as we were led to suppose, and had they known our position, they might have captured the whole column without firing a shot.

D*

The ribbon of land on which we had our bivouac could be swept by a battery planted at the head of the bridge — which was the only way of egress, while the place was too narrow to manœuvre a platoon even. A small detachment of cavalry dashing through our line of pickets might have sprung the trap upon us before we could have extricated ourselves. But as good luck would have it the enemy were nowhere near us, being well on their way to Gettysburg. Though the force whose presence near Carlisle alarmed our commander and induced him to countermarch the column, was, as already stated, no more than a small cavalry escort of a rebel train of plunder on its way to the main rebel army, yet it is probable that the large cavalry force of General Stuart was not far off; for Stuart had been detached, as General Lee states in his report of this his second Cis-Potomac campaign, "to follow the movements of the Federal army south of the Potomac after our own (rebel) had entered Maryland."

On that Thursday afternoon while our small column was loitering on the Carlisle road, our backs turned upon that city, the terrible struggle was renewed at Gettysburg, closing at sunset — about the time we came to a halt in the romantic vale of the Conedoguinet for our night's bivouac, supposing the enemy to be within striking distance of us!

Friday.—Up at half-past three o'clock, and on the march at five, after having braced ourselves for a solid day's work with hot coffee and bread, or hard tack and butter—the bread and butter being the fruit of yesterday's foraging. Some even fared on chicken, goose, lamb, etc., though it is feared the rightful owners thereof were not always invited to the feast.

Emerging from the valley we set our faces again toward Carlisle ; and being disencumbered of knapsacks and woolen blankets, which were ordered to be brought forward in wagons, we jogged along in fine spirits. This light marching order, as the phrase is, involves a weight of some thirty pounds, musket included. At ten o'clock, having advanced some seven miles, our regiment was halted in a grove just out of the village of Kinston, for a noon-rest. By the persuasive force of greenbacks the villagers and outlying farmers were induced to unearth a goodly supply of bread, butter and eggs, hidden relentlessly doubtless from the holders of confederate shinplasters during the late sojourn of King Jeff's hungry subjects. Cherry pies were also added to our regimental bill of fare, which was due to the energies of an enterprising officer who had them baked for us and brought in hot! There had been no issuance of rations since we left Bridgeport Heights, and accordingly each company had to depend for supplies on its enterprise in foraging. This was a lesson easily learned and daily improved upon, though many a poor fellow, doubtless, of less adroit companies, had spare diet oftener than he considered was healthy. We sprinkled ourselves over the grove in knots or alone, and slept, sang, read, wrote, rambled, eat and drank, or did whatever other thing was most pleasing to ourselves.

About one o'clock we again took up our line of march. The sun was blazing fiercely, there was but little breeze, and the danger of sunstroke to many of us was imminent. But as the emergency was pressing and orders peremptory, the column was pushed along with but short rests, and we made Carlisle safely at sunset, having travelled since morning some thirteen miles. We were halted in a field near the town, and found no other traces of the visit of an enemy than the ruins of the United States barracks, and a few carcasses of horses near us. The condition of these latter made it necessary as a sanitary precaution to cover them with earth. Accordingly spade parties were quickly detailed for this service.

"The Valley"—as this whole region is known to the inhabitants thereof — through the midst of which our road lay, is one of the most beautiful farming countries imaginable. Vast reaches of level, now golden with grain, stretch from the Blue Ridge on the west to the Blue Mountains on the east, eight to ten miles apart. Looking over the country from any point of the road the things one sees at this period of the year which fix themselves in the memory, are grain, granaries and mountains; the whole scene suggesting the Happy Valley of Amhara, the prescriptive residence of Rasselas and the other princes of Abyssinia. The barns are surprising structures, though of a piece with the country. Such fields need and presuppose such granaries. They are usually built of brick or stone, of huge dimensions, having sheds near the ground as a cover for cattle. In the distance they loom up like vast warehouses, completely dwarfing the adjacent farm-houses. Many of the residences we found deserted; and of those that were occupied but few gave us greeting. But the welcome of this few was so hearty and substantial as to put us in a humor to forgive the meanness of the rest.

While we were making our morning march, the hostile armies at Gettysburg were ordering their lines for a resumption of battle ; and at the moment of our emergence from the woods where we had our delightful noon-rest, that tremendous fire of artillery from " over one hundred and twenty-five guns," opened upon the Union army, preparatory to the last grand assault, which was made while we were on our way to Carlisle; the disastrous repulse of which terminated the contest, and left the heroic Army of the Potomac master of the field.

Fourth of July.—At 3 A.M. we were called up to resume our march. The previous day had been a trying one to us, and our bivouac was refreshing accordingly. As we marched through Carlisle we greeted the day with patriotic airs without exciting the slightest demonstration beyond an occasional waving of a handkerchief. The people gathered to see us pass, looking on listlessly. We did not notice a rag of bunting flying except our own colors, though it was the nation's birth-day!

We turned down the road leading to Mount Holly Gap, a pass in South Mountain. Five miles out we got a fine view of the range we were to cross. It rose a couple of miles ahead of us, like a Cyclopean wall, running directly athwart our path. At the base of it nestled Papertown ; but as yet only the brown church spire and a few housetops were visible against the back-ground of the blue mountain. At this village we were greeted for the first time on our march with cheers! But perhaps the people had an especially strong motive for feeling patriotic and demonstrative, Stuart's cavalry having passed through a day or two before, on its way to join the main rebel army at Gettysburg. The road was paved with their hoof prints.

Entering the gap we shortly came upon a mountain stream which flowed along the road-side, and here we were permitted to stop and bathe our travel-bruised feet. But our business was urgent, and we were soon in line again pressing on up the mountain. When eight or nine miles distant from Carlisle we halted for a noon rest. At this point the two lips of the gap approach at the base within one hundred feet of each other—two-thirds of which space is occupied by the brook, and the remainder, for the most part, by the road. This place is a Thermopylae, but being only a side-door of the State of Pennsylvania, no step had been taken to close it against invaders. The day was beautiful, and we stretched ourselves along the shady bank to rest, sleep, write, nibble on our hard tack, or do whatever pleased us best. All about us being

"A forest primeval,"

there was no near chance for foraging, and so we all rested. Some with surprising versatility improvised hook and line, and went a-fishing—their luck ranging from a nibble to the smallest variety of minnow. Others equally enterprising hunted for blackberries in places where a blackberry would have been frightened to death to find itself growing—whether they climbed trees for them is not positively known.

Reports now began to come in of a great battle going on, of which we had abundant proof before the day was ended. Up to this time our campaign had been quite an innocent one; and though we had had some wearisome marching, yet benignant skies had uniformly attended us. But now all was to be suddenly changed. First came the hot rumors of battle, and we realized the urgency of the moment, and wondered whether we should be in time to help in our feeble way to win the great victory we hoped for, little dreaming that the contest was already decided—the great victory already won. Next came clouded skies; and as we rested, there rose to our ears the distant mutter of thunder, and soon big drops began to fall. Presently a mist was seen to gather around the top of the mountain far above our heads; and soon the top disappeared in the shroud which crept ominously down, down the mountain side. We began to think of shelter, and unrolled our overcoats and rubber cloths. The thunder grew louder, the lightning flashed more and more vividly and the rain fell in torrents. A poor little cabin on the roadside gave shelter to a few. A leaky shed treacherously invited others. Some seemed to think it unsoldier-like to shrink before the elements, and doggedly grinned and bore it. But the greater part of us crouched to the ground under the trees, hauling our rubber blankets over our heads so as to shed the rain. Like the victims of the first deluge, we suspected it would not be much of a shower, and were only less mistaken than those wretched beings.

Over against the mountain wall before and above us there hung in mid-air a vast sheet of water which the howling wind flapped to and fro in the gorge terrifically; while the blinding lightning and crashing thunder seemed to issue together from the mountain itself. The creek, before clear and placid, quickly became turgid and agitated. It began to creep up the banks. Presently a dark, strange-looking mass came floating down — it was a soldier's knapsack! The rain fell, if possible, in increased torrents. The stream continued to rise rapidly. Other knapsacks came floating down. It was not long before the water stood two feet above its former level. Would it keep on raining till it flooded the road and us? For two hours the rain poured down with only momentary abatement to renew itself as furiously as before. The calm mountain brook had become a raging torrent, threatening the whole gorge with overflow, carrying angrily down a stream of knapsacks, officers' valises, etc. As we afterward found, the torrent had caught them where they had been piled together; the rising water having isolated them and put them beyond the reach of their owners.

There being no signs of the storm abating the order came to "Forward." We fell in resignedly and even with good humor, having by this time got pretty thoroughly soaked—every expedient of shelter failing; indeed we had given up trying to keep dry, and many of us had taken to sauntering up and down the road watching the baggage drift by, and laughing to see one another's forlorn appearance. With trailing arms we marched cheerily up the mountain, singing with infinite gusto, "Marching along," "John Brown" and kindred airs — our choruses sounding out grandly in that wild place, and amid that terrific storm. A little further on we came to a manufacturing hamlet in a sort of cup of the mountain, the stream on which the mill stood flowing over the edge of the cup at one side as it were. At this point, or near it, we left the Carlisle pike and took the mountain road on our right, following up the course of the Mountain Creek. We now began to fall in with a stream of men, dressed in U.S. uniform, but without arms. They reported themselves to be paroled prisoners captured in Wednesday's battle of Gettysburg. They told us the battle was still raging and that we should soon be in the midst of it. This was definite, the first definite information we had had from the Army of the Potomac, since we began our march. We were now convinced that a great battle was going on, or had just been fought, and whether lost or won, we felt we must be needed. This news animated every bosom — some with anxiety — some with courage; and we pressed on with renewed vigor.

Two miles further on, at the point where Hunter's Run crosses the road, the column was delayed on account of some obstruction in front. Working our way along slowly we presently came in sight of the trouble. It was a sea of water, covering the road waist-deep, in which men and horses were seen to be floundering promiscuously. A portion of the column succeeded in getting through, though at imminent peril of being washed away and it was thought prudent to postpone further attempts at crossing till the water subsided. A countermarch was accordingly ordered to the paper mill, which being deserted gave us ample quarters. It was an extensive establishment, and looked as if work had been suspended unexpectedly and suddenly. Here were great bins of rags washed and sorted ready for conversion; here vats of bleached pulp, like snow-drifts; here piles of white paper, as it dropped from the calender, with a sheet hanging half issued. We built fires, dried our clothes, cooked coffee — the little we had left — and regaled ourselves as best he could with the assistance of a morsel of hard tack which the rain had reduced to semi-pulp — though of this delicious viand many of us had not a sample. The hamlet could furnish us but a very limited supply of creature comforts, the rebels having got there ahead of us, and made themselves quite at home in kitchen and larder. About 5 P.M., the rain having ceased, though the skies still threatened, we again took up the line of march, leaving behind several poor fellows, whom the march had put *hors de combat*, quartered among the good people of the place.

On again reaching the point of danger we found the water had subsided but little; but orders were imperative, and we plunged in. The passage was perilous. The road lay along the side of the mountain down which the stream poured in a torrent, unseen till it came roaring out of the forest at the roadside, surging furiously across the road, and disappearing down the tangled wood on the opposite side with the roar of a cataract. A distance of not more than a hundred feet of its course was visible. We heard it coming, saw it rush by us, and heard its awful leap into the depths of the wilderness again. It was the leap of a tiger from covert to covert across a traveller's path; or like a hyena at night, disclosed only by the glare of his eyeballs.

We followed the trail cautiously feeling our way along, and not daring to look to the right or left—our ears filled with the din of the waters, and half carried off our feet by the impetuous flood. Crossing a gully — probably the natural bed of the stream — by a foot bridge, which our engineers had doubtless thrown across, we saw beneath us with a start and a shudder of horror the head of a drowned horse and the pole of a wagon sticking up above the torrent. All else was out of sight. It proved to be a loaded commissary wagon with its team, which had been swept away! A number of muskets were lost, and a drum or two; but excepting these casualties we all got across safely with no other ill fortune than to be wet again to the skin, which, as night was falling gave us a comfortless prospect. The drum corps of the Twenty-Third was at this point sent back to Carlisle with the remainder of the drums, thirteen in number.

In this part of the mountain the road runs level for several miles along its slope, and being cut down on both sides is for long distances little better than a ditch. The soil being a stiff clay, the tremendous rain-fall having insufficient escape converted the road into a canal—six inches to a foot of water overlying six inches to a foot of mire. And into this infernal passage we plunged as night closed upon us. For a couple of hours we floundered along with desperate energy, losing shoes sucked off by the tenacious slime, and some even throwing away their blankets. It was pitch dark; it had begun to rain again; we were hungry—having had nothing but a little wet hard tack and one small ration of coffee since we left Carlisle—and many, many of us not so much; we were very jaded, having marched already a dozen miles, much of it up the mountain, and much of it through mud that would challenge the admiration of a veteran of the Army of the Potomac; and the floods of air and earth had soaked us to the skin. Still we kept up our courage and pressed forward; for now we had reason to believe that a great battle was raging, which would, we hoped, be decisive of the salvation of the Republic, and we prayed that if any exigency had arisen or should arise — which seemed not improbable — in which the militia reserve should be needed to turn the fortunes of the day in favor of our arms, we might not be too late.

Some three miles beyond Hunter's Run we passed a poor cabin — the first human tenement we had seen since leaving the Mount Holley paper mill. Pitch darkness was now fallen upon us. Here were gathered a motley crowd of stragglers — thirty or forty in number — from regiments in advance of us. They had built fires in different parts of the premises, and looked, as they sat and stood huddled around them, like gipsies — their faces red in the ghastly fire-light. Some were moving about under the trees of the door-yard, like phantoms. At a short distance in rear of the cabin thin parallel streaks of light were visible, as if shining through the chinks of a barn. Here, it was evident, another squad was quartered. As we passed this group of shadows, and plunged again into the gloomy darkness, the spectral sight, as we looked back, seemed like a phantasmagoria of Hades.

A mile further and we halted—a thicket along the roadside offering a retreat only less forlorn than the miry road. Rubber cloths were spread and we lay down for a little sleep. But the work of the day was not yet ended. About midnight we were roused again by the order "Forward column!"—a forced march indeed! The exigency, it was evident, must be great! On, on, through rain and mire, one mile, two miles, three miles to the hamlet of Laurel Forge, indistinguishable in the darkness, which gave refuge to all that remained of what was twelve hours before a proud regiment, filling the mountains with the echoes of its fervid patriotic song, now a forlorn, exhausted handful of men clutching greedily the shelter and the hope of rest which the grimy forge offered. From this category must be excepted one company which, occupying the right of the column, had forced the passage of the flood at Hunter's Run when we first reached it on our march, the imminent peril attending which had caused the order of countermarch to be given to the rest of the regiment. They reached the dusky hamlet before dark and passed the night in comparative comfort.

Thus closed at Laurel Forge—now forever associated in our memories with the Valley Forge of

the Fathers by reason of a common suffering—
our Fourth of July in the wilderness. If those
immortal patriots who gave us the day fared worse
for our sakes, we who kept the day are content to
know that we fared about as badly as was in our
power for the sake of those who are to follow us.
To think of friends at home setting off rockets
and the like in honor of the day, and very likely in
our honor too, seemed so ridiculous in connection
with our sorry plight as to provoke laughter irre-
sistibly. It was like trying to cheer a mourning
friend at a funeral by telling him stories.

To sum up our Fourth of July work:—Distance
travelled, including the countermarch, half of it
through frightful mire, *seventeen miles;* weight
carried, allowing for the additional weight given
to overcoat, tents and clothes by their being soaked
through and through a good deal of the time,
thirty-two and a half pounds; with insufficent food,
and bad feet under most of us.

At Gettysburg there was a cessation of hostilities
throughout the day, both armies remaining in
position, apparently taking a breathing spell preparatory to renewing the struggle on the morrow.
During the night, however, the rebel retreat began
by the Fairfield road. The rear of the column did
not get away till after daylight on the 5th.

Sunday, July 5th.—In the early morning, which it were a satire to call the Sabbath day, as it had seemed ridiculous to us to think of the day before being the jubilee day of our boyhood, we scratched open our eyes and looked about us to see what sort of a place it was we had fallen upon. Half a dozen small, unpainted, dingy wooden cabins stuck along the road-side, an iron furnace and a few other buildings, appendages of the latter, or nondescripts, greeted our sight. But there was one thing we saw which made us glad — a fine mill-stream, where though the water was turbid and yellow we bathed, and washed the mud and grit out of our clothes. Some of us found in the miserable settlement a little coffee and some flour, the latter of which we were at no loss how to use—for what soldier has not heard of flap-jack? Entering a cabin, and taking possession of the family cooking stove—the women of the establishment meekly withdrawing—a small party of us prepared our repast. One brought water from a neighboring spring; another mixed the dough; another fed the fire from the wood-pile in the corner; another found a dish-cloth and swabbed off the top of the stove preparatory to laying on the dough; for we thought of our sweethearts, and our mothers and sisters, and could not endure the idea of dirty cookery! Then we spread out the ready paste flat on the place appointed to receive it, where it went to cooking at once with most obliging promptitude. We sat around the stove, on the wood-pile, on chairs, on stools, on baby's cradle, on the floor.

Another crowd, having no pecuniary interest in the transaction, formed an outer circle, accommodated with standees. All watched the growing prodigy in silence and with greedy eyes. First it began to brown around the edges. Then it began to puff up. After that the swelling went down again, leaving the surface all wrinkled like the face of a monkey. Then a fine smoke rose from it, as it were, incense. Could it be "done"? and was this the sign from the gods? Perhaps; at any rate it was the sign of something; probably the sign of scorching on the under side. Then it ought to be turned. But how turned? Ah, how, indeed! It had been easy to spread it on—but the turning!

> "Facilis descensus Averni;
> Noctes atque dies patet atri janua Ditis;
> Sed revocare gradum, superasque evadere ad auras.
> Hoc opus, his labor est."

A knife was brought; too short and too narrow. A spoon; better, but still inadequate. An outsider suggested that all hands lay hold of the thing on one side and flop it over suddenly. But the jealous proprietors demurred, fearing that the movement might not be simultaneous and that thus a flap-jack rupture might ensue, followed by possible skedaddling of the shrewd operators bearing off the spoil. Meanwhile the smoke was alarmingly on the increase and something must be done at once. While we were in this quandary, the principal partner in the concern, a long, lank fellow with tong-like fingers, in a fit of desperation seized the thing in one hand with an old rag, and over it went k-e-r-f-l-o-p! The danger was past, and we congratulated the skillful operator and one another on the auspicious result. Mr. Flapjack after that proceeded soberly to do himself brown, whereupon we all partook, smearing each mouthful with molasses which a miraculous cupboard furnished, and pronounced it good—in fact excellent. At home not one of us but would as soon think of eating the stove itself, both as to cleanliness and digestibility.

While we were recuperating at Laurel Forge on that strange Sabbath morning a constant stream of stragglers and fragmentary companies of different regiments were coming in. One of them reported meeting a party on the road whose situation very fairly represented the degree of wretchedness which all—officers and men alike—underwent on that eventful day and night of the Fourth of July. It was just at daybreak. The men were wading along through the mire as a staff officer rode by and drew rein at the roadside a little ahead of them, in front of a party of some three or four officers who were evidently having their bivouac there in miserable isolation. The officer whom the messenger saluted as his superior was bare-headed, having evidently just risen from the ground where his rubber cloth and blanket still lay. His dress was wet and begrimed with mud; his hair was frowsy, lying in ropy tangles upon his head and hanging over his brows; and his face was haggard with anxiety and suffering. It was Brigadier-General———; and here in this solitary wilderness had actually been his bivouac, in company with a few of his staff. Taking what was overheard as a clue, something like the following colloquy passed between the messenger and the General:

"General, a complete company, or anything like it cannot be found on the road—much less a regiment of the brigade. They are scattered everywhere—sick, exhausted, famished: and if they were together, they could not be fed." "Where are the wagons?" "Stuck in the mud, sir, miles back. The teams are broken down and others cannot be procured. I don't see how we can possibly get the wagons up." "Ah, * * * h'm, * * * Did you see no farmers' houses around anywhere?" "The country here, sir, is a perfect wilderness. The only habitations are a few cabins of poor people, scattered along the road at long intervals; and even of these there is but one for the whole seven or eight miles between the paper mill and Laurel Forge."

It was palpable enough that the situation was alarming. The column broken up into a vast stream of stragglers — regiments and brigades mixed promiscuously together — men and officers half-famished, jaded out, buried in the depths of a mountain wilderness—the subsistence trains mired far in the rear and no prospect of their getting up; all this rushing at once upon the mind of a conscientious commander wholly unused to the hardships of real campaigning, and before he had had time to throw off the incubus of the dismal night he must have endured, was enough to crush any but a heroic spirit.

The skeleton of the Twenty-Third having gone forward early in the morning, our little private "breakfast party" hastened its departure from the now to us historic hamlet of Laurel Forge, after gratifying the poor woman who presided over the dingy domicil with the sight of more money in her hands, doubtless, than she was accustomed to seeing at one time. The road now began to improve at once. We were getting "out of the wilderness" apparently. A few miles brought us to Pine Grove, another settlement with its furnace and shops. Then shortly after we began to ascend again; and we wondered with fear and trembling whether we were entering upon a second mountain road which it would be our wretched fate to climb. There rose indeed before us, two or three miles off, a formidable range whose crest must have towered well nigh a thousand feet above us; and though it did not lie directly across the path we were going, the road bent suspiciously toward it. We had little strength left for such a renewal of our toils. Up — up — up; nearer and nearer the crest of the mountain, till it became at length evident that we were actually on its flank, and that our road lay over its very top. The rain had ceased, the sun was fighting his way out from among torn clouds, and the air was sultry. The road was filled with a vast stream of stragglers intermixed with officers on horseback, and wagons. Along the roadside weary soldiers were resting. Here one had fallen out alone, exhausted and disheartened, and another coming up had sat down beside him on the greensward for a moment, though wearing the uniform of a different regiment. The latter, with a true soldier's feeling, was giving the poor fellow a drink from his canteen, and administering the cheap but precious solace of kind and encouraging words, while big tears rolled down the cheeks of the other. Such scenes were frequently observed. Common sufferings had broken down all barriers and we felt for one another the tenderness of brothers.

Slowly and wearily we toiled on — one mile — two miles. The road stretched up steep and stony. It was a comfort to be rid of the mire, but the stones were afflicting enough to our bruised feet. How the batteries were ever dragged up that mountain road so soon after emerging from those miles and miles of mire is one of the wonders of equine endurance. But so it was. We found on the summit that incomparable Philadelphia Battery which had accompanied us from the fort, and had won golden opinions from all by the unfailing promptitude and uncomplaining endurance with which the little company had borne more than their share of toil and privation. At the top of the mountain the road was blocked up for long distances with infantry and artillery at a halt; and here a good portion of our stragglers came up with the now rehabilitated regiment. The enemy was reported to be near. What enemy or in what force we could not learn. This much, however, was understood;—the Eleventh Brigade, or all that was left of it was ordered to the front! At length the order "Forward" ran along the line, and on we marched again. We soon came to a cross-roads in an open wood. Here cannon were planted to command both approaches, hid in front by leafy branches of trees laid up against them. These were masked batteries, and it was to be our duty to support them. This looked like business. One hundred rods or so further brought us to a pretty opening where we were halted and ordered to pitch tents in the adjoining timber. Foragers were at once despatched, great fires built, tents pitched, and preparations made for such supper as was possible under the circumstances, just as if our pleasant arrangements were not liable to be stopped at any moment by the appearance of the enemy. But we were too exhausted to feel nervous with anxiety. At length the foragers returned with gratifying reports, the substantial fruits of which were fresh bread and butter, together with a supply of live stock next morning. During the night the commissary wagons came up, and in the morning we had coffee once more, and new rations of hard-tack were given out.

E*

The 5th was spent by Lee at Gettysburg in making good his escape, a large portion of his immense trains moving by the Cashtown road guarded by a force of cavalry under General Imboden. As soon as General Meade discovered the enemy's retreat he sent General Sedgwick with the Sixth Corps in pursuit; but the latter was not able to accomplish much.

Monday, 6th.—Our approach and preparations to meet the enemy had not developed his presence, though some straggling rebels were brought in who had been picked up by our scouts in the mountains, to whom they had given themselves up without resistance. Accordingly about the middle of the forenoon we were ordered to advance again. Some of us had cherished the hope that we would be permitted to rest over Monday; for we sorely needed it, and felt that, should we be marched then into the van of battle—what with our physical exhaustion and our wasted ranks—we could make but a poor show of fight. But it seemed the exigency was too urgent to admit of delay. We therefore pulled up stakes again, strapped our luggage to our backs, shouldered our pieces, and marched forward in the direction of Gettysburg.

A hard march of fifteen miles over a rough mountain road that pretty much all the time went up or down, and occasionally by long stretches, brought the column to Cashtown, a cross-roads settlement, ten miles north-west from Gettysburg, where the mountain road meets the Gettysburg and Chambersburg pike. Here we bivouacked in an orchard. This place is memorable to the Twenty-Third regiment on account of a sad disaster there befalling, in which one of our number was the unhappy actor. He fired off a musket charged with ball cartridge, supposing he was only snapping a cap, directly into the ranks of the Twenty-Eighth regiment of our brigade, wounding two men—one of them mortally. No sooner was the lamentable event known to the regiment than they took instant steps to make the only reparation in their power. They subscribed on the spot a purse of some twelve hundred dollars, which they duly paid, for the relief of the families of the victims.

We had thought to make this spot memorable in a very different and happier way, viz., by the capture of the rebel train bearing the precious spoils which the enemy had taken from our people. But we were too late; it had all got safely past before we came up. That furious storm which had broken over us in the mountains, rendering the roads impassable or extremely difficult, had been the agent of Providence to hold us back.

However disposed on the spur of the moment and in the vexation of disappointment we may have felt to regard our delay as an unmitigated misfortune, depriving us of a golden opportunity of earning a direct share, however small, in the glories of Gettysburg, still we may be sure a wiser hand than ours guided the issues of those memorable days. It is probable that the cavalry force of Imboden, guarding that important train, was large; at any rate large enough to have trampled out our handful of men had we made an attack. Had the skies favored we could hardly have reached Cashtown a day sooner than we did without making forced marches; much straggling must have ensued; and the column thus reduced would have come up in an exhausted condition. To be sure we might have harassed the enemy, caused confusion among the teams, and perhaps destroyed or compelled him to destroy a part of his train. But we were too late, and speculation or regret is now unavailing.

When General Meade despatched Sedgwick's corps in pursuit of the flying enemy on the Fairfield road, he sent at the same time a force of cavalry on the Cashtown road to capture or destroy the rebel train. They "captured," in the words of Lee himself, "a number of wagons and ambu-

ances; but they (the rebel wagon train) succeeded
n reaching Williamsport without serious loss."
Sedgwick appears to have been unsuccessful in
eriously harassing the retreat of Lee, the Fair-
ield pass, up to which place he pushed the pur-
uit, being so strong a natural position as to enable
a small force holding it to check for a considerable
ime any pursuing foe. General Meade remained
at Gettysburg with the bulk of the army during
he 5th and 6th, " engaged in succoring the wounded and burying the dead."

Sunday, 7th.—Our attempted exploit of captur-
ng or destroying the enemy's train having thus
miscarried, we resumed the chase, taking the
Chambersburg pike. In thus turning our backs
upon Gettysburg, whither we supposed we were
bound, we might naturally wonder " what next?"
That this supposition was correct, witness the fol-
owing order:

"(Pine Grove), July 7th, (6th), 1863.

In compliance with Division Orders this command
will take up line of march for Gettysburg forthwith.

This Brigade will take the advance — regiments in
he following order:—7th, 8th, 56th, 52nd, 23rd.

*   *   *   *   *   *

By order of
J. C. SMITH,
Brigadier-General Commanding.

We followed the Chambersburg pike as far as Greenwood where we turned to the left down a road leading southerly. The remains of a caisson and a forge which had been knocked to pieces so as to be unserviceable to the finder, and unused rifle shells scattered along the road indicated the haste of the retreat of the enemy. To facilitate their escape they had moved in two columns, one by the road, the other through the adjoining fields, where the ripe grain for long distances lay trampled for the breadth of the line.

About 4 P. M., we came to a halt in a grove just out of the little village of Altodale, (erroneously called Functown by Col. VARIAN of the 8th and Col. TRAFFORD of the 71st in their published reports of the campaign), having accomplished a distance of some fourteen miles from Cashtown. Here we realized more keenly than we had yet done that we were coming upon classic ground. Through the grove flowed a brawling brook named the Little Antietam. The waters which there soothed our travel-bruised feet and refreshed our weary limbs were destined to bathe the historic field where the patriot army hurled back the first rebel invasion. But the neighborhood is itself memorable for a prior transaction, connected with one of the most pregnant events in the history of the

country. Near the place of our bivouac, John E.
Cook, one of the unfortunate confederates of John
Brown of Harper's Ferry, was arrested. Cook,
it will be remembered, escaped from Harper's
Ferry by taking to the mountains of Maryland on
foot; and after having reached a spot where he
expected to find sympathizing friends, was treacherously seized by one Logan, and sent back to a
Virginia gallows. This execrated wretch now
lives, poor and despised by his neighbors, in this
village of Altodale. But it is pleasant to be able
to say that his wife, as if an atoning angel,
opened her doors, (Logan was absent on a distant
journey at the time), and showed to our men —
they being ignorant of who their entertainer was
— a generous hospitality. She fed the hungry and
nursed the sick with christian charity.

On this Tuesday morning the entire rebel army
reached Hagerstown; and at the same moment
General Meade set on foot from Gettysburg a flank
movement by way of Middletown.

The skies threatening we pitched tents for the
night along the Little Antietam. Toward morning the rain fell furiously. It dripped through
the canvas above us, it crept in under the edges of
the tents, and soaked the rubber cloths on which
we lay. When our situation under cover had be-

come sufficiently miserable, seized with insane impatience we crawled out into the open air, only to find that our neighbors had been as insane as ourselves. It was then early daybreak. You could dimly see, gathered around the faintly burning embers of the company fires, a few strange-looking objects, black and utterly shapeless except near the ground where a pair of legs protruded. As you moved through the wood you everywhere met forms like these wandering about aimlessly and in moody silence. Squat on the ground were others —mere black shapeless heaps. Some were collected around the trunks of trees. Some were scattered about on rocks and stumps. Wherever you went they were directly in front and on either side of you. As the beams of morning crept through the grove the phantasmagoria became still more striking. Distant objects were brought to light, and those near you, faintly descried or not observed before, became distinct. The whole extended wood was seen to be filled with these black shapeless heaps, strewn on the ground indiscriminately everywhere. They encircled the smouldering fires, which ever and anon would shoot up a sparkling blaze as if some one had stirred them. Some taller than the rest were moving about slowly and solemnly. Here and there were commissary and quartermaster wagons, the teams unhitched and turned about like Barnum's equine monster—their heads where their tails ought to be—and looking demurely into the wagons, where, on boxes and barrels, were other dismal black heaps. Observe one of these. It is crowned with a soft felt hat, the rim bent down all around, from which the water is dripping drearily. Looking under it you see the large, sad, careworn visage of Colonel Everdell, ever watchful of his men, and now sharing with them this extremity of discomfort and exposure.

As the morning waxes light the camp-fires flame up stronger if not brighter, and now you see real human figures moving about. These ominous black heaps scattered everywhere are, as it were, eggs, and out of each of them will crawl in due time a full-fledged biped. See yonder by that fire; one of them is even now in violent motion—evidently in the pangs of birth. Presto! a man emerges from it as it collapses to the ground. He goes straight to the fire, stirs it up, blows the sick embers, cuts slivers for kindling and lays them on, takes the axe, splits a rail in pieces which he piles on the now quivering spires of flame, and goes to other black heaps and shakes them with reproachful summons. Lo, these too split apart, and out from each appears a man! These take black iron pots and go off. Presently they come swinging back with the pots filled with water. Meantime the fire is finely started, the pots are slung astride a long pole set over the fire, the wood crackles, the flames shoot up wrapping the pots around. And now the camp is all astir. The black objects are twice as numerous as before, moving about with increased animation. You imagine Little Antietam to be the Acheron of fable, and all these to be poor ghosts, strangely clad in the mortal habiliments of woe, crowding the banks of the fateful river, and waiting, sick with hope deferred, their turn to cross; and your eyes wander curiously along the swollen, dashing stream to catch sight of the unclean grizzly beard, Charon, the ferryman, and his crazy skiff:—

> "There stands
> Charon, who rules the dreary coast—
> A sordid god: down from his hoary chin
> A length of beard descends, uncomb'd, unclean:
> * * * *
> He spreads his canvas; with his pole he steers;
> The freight of flitting ghosts in his thin bottom bears
> * * * *
> An airy crowd came rushing where he stood,
> Which filled the margin of the fateful flood—
> * * * *

> Thick as the leaves in autumn strew the woods,
> Or fowls, by winter forced, forsake the floods,
> And wing their hasty flight to happier lands—
> Such and so thick the shiv'ring army stands,
> And press for passage with extended hands.
> Now these, now those, the surly boatman bore :
> The rest he drove to distance from the shore.
>
> * * * *
>
> A hundred years they wander on the shore ;
> At length, their penance done, are wafted o'er."

Then you fancy them a collection of howling dervishes; or a congregation of monks in Purgatory, the figures about the fires being the working devils preparing to roast the poor monks for their morning's course of expiatory torment.

While you are trying to drown your misery in this sort of musing the fire is doing its work, and soon the pots boil, the fixens are tossed in, and the coffee. Near by your own company fire—that is what most interests you now—there is spread on the ground a rubber cloth, whose irregular protuberant shape suggests agreeable things. The busy figure at the fire approaches the mystery, raises the covering at one end and draws forth bread, which he cuts in chunks, loaf after loaf; a crock of apple butter — a Pennsylvanian Dutch dish somewhat analagous to the apple sauce of the Yankees; and a can of brown sugar — a luxury which only the prudent forethought of enterprising officers rendered possible, intended doubtless for their own mess, but generously devoted to the comfort of the company, now struggling under the terrible triple load of fatigue, privation and exposure. For be it remembered that, although we had had fresh meat rations served out to us only forty-eight hours previously, sufficient to last us a couple of days if not wasted, yet the unexpectedness and suddenness of our resumption of the march had prevented us, in our inexperience, from availing ourselves of the provision. Indeed it rarely happened that we carried in our haversacks from bivouac to bivouac anything more than half a dozen hard-tack, if so many, which we snatched up hastily as we fell into line for the forward march. So that the only real refreshment we found within our reach at the end of each day's march, when, weary, hungry and sore we dropt down on the rough ground of bivouac, was night itself and its sweet gift of sleep. Whatever may be the theories of physiologists on the subject, we felt, as a matter of daily experience, that a good, wholesome, appetizing meal half an hour or an hour after coming to a halt would have enabled us to endure much harder marches with much less fatigue than is here recorded.

All being ready, the boiling pots are slipped off the fire, and the viands set on the ground in order before the master of ceremonies. A shout goes forth, "Fall in for rations!" But the call is needless. For the last half hour fifty pairs of eyes have been following every motion of the cook and his volunteer aids, and tin plates and cups been giving forth their dulcet strains. A long cue of black headless devils stands merry before the flourishing disciple of Soyer. He dips into the smoking pot of stew and raises a cupful, dripping and delicious; a plate is ready to receive it. He dips again; another is ready. The supernumeraries dispense the coffee, bread, apple-butter, and sweetnin'. The black cue shortens one by one till the last hungry devil is supplied, and all have assumed the squat posture, and the grove is filled with black heaps again. But not now as before. Then all were glum, silent, motionless — the rain pelting them remorselessly. Now every one is alive with movement and talk. By and bye the weather clears up a little. One after another, human forms reappear upon the scene. The drummers sound their call;—it is the Assembly—the summons to forward march. Tents are struck quickly: luggage rolled and shouldered; arms taken; and away goes an army of brave youths, three short hours ago utterly and miserably "played out", now ready to make a long day's march, or to move upon the enemy, singing as they pass under Logan's windows, " Marching along," " John Brown," etc., ignorant at the moment of the poetic justice which their mighty chorus celebrates.

A member of the Twenty-Third left behind at Altodale, sick and in care of a kind mater-familias, related an amusing experience which illustrates the semi-civilization of the people of those regions. His bed was provided with but one sheet; and the hostess kindly enquired whether he would rather have a counterpane or a blanket next him—"some people prefers one, and some the other!" she remarked. He thanked her blandly and chose the counterpane. During the two days and nights of his stay he did not hear the sound of a piano, nor a note of music from the inhabitants, though he was in the heart of the village, and at twilight saw young ladies promenading the street. In lively contrast to this neglect of the divine gift of music, he heard, on the second evening, a company of soldiers who were dallying in the place, singing patriotic songs. which were received by their comrades with a familiar " Hi! Hi! " This sudden irruption of democratic New York into a Pennsylvania Dutch village, whose only idea of the great city was, doubtless, what had been derived from rose-colored descriptions and fanciful pictures of its great hotels or its streets of palaces, must have seemed to the inhabitants about as strange as the unheralded appearance on Broadway, some fine afternoon, of a caravan of Bedouins from Arabia.

Another instance was narrated to show the primitive taste of the villagers; one more to the point than that just recorded, which may have been accidental. Opposite the room where he lay sick was the residence of one of the rich men of the place. His house was of brick, commodious and painfully plain. The roadway extended to the very door, the only marks of division between the portion to be used for vehicles and that intended as a walk being a locust tree and a bridle post. The door was raised some two feet above the ground, and was reached by a partly hewn log, from around which the rain had washed away quite a depth of gravel, so that it now presented an awkward step for a lady. Though there was abundant room for a door yard there was no enclosure, no sign of shrub or flower. Here dwelt one of the upper-tendom of Altodale.

This same soldier, on his way to rejoin his regiment met a Pennsylvania youngster with whom he had the following colloquy: —

"Many more back?" inquired the boy, who evidently wanted to know whether there were many more troops coming forward. Carlyle might envy such terseness of language.

"No, not many. Did many pass here yesterday?"

"No, not so very many. But last night there was quite a *drove of 'em*."

This language was either not complimentary to the discipline of the New York militia while on the march, or not complimentary to the schoolmasters of Franklin County, Pa. Imagine such a conversation in a rural district of Massachusetts!

As an offset to this promising lad, he heard of another who was chopping wood by the roadside when the rebel army was passing. One of the rascally tatterdemalions coming close to him made a grab for his hat — it was a fashion they had of helping themselves to the head-gear of everybody they passed — but missed it. The boy turned, raised his axe, and "dared" the rebel "to try that again!"

From Altodale the column followed the course of the Little Antietam in a south-westerly direction to Waynesboro', and came to camp two miles beyond on the Waynesboro' and Hagerstown pike. The day was pleasantly cool, and the march of eleven miles was made in comparative comfort, notwithstanding the roads were heavy and our wet luggage and clothes added greatly to our burden. As to rations we were learning to get along with the scantiest supply, like the horse of the enterprising economist which was trained to subsist at last on one oat a day, and was on the point of getting along on nothing when he unexpectedly gave up the ghost. Whether our lot would have been similar had our term of service continued a few days longer can never be positively known.

At Waynesboro' we fell in with the Sixth Corps of the army, which, as before mentioned, had been despatched by General Meade from the field of Gettysburg, on the 5th instant, in pursuit of the enemy by the Fairfield Road—their line of march being thus nearly parallel to ours. Here we were, then, in the midst of the world-renowned Army of the Potomac—in fact incorporated with it, being now subject to the orders, as we understood, of that gallant soldier, Major-General Sedgwick, who fought his corps so splendidly at Fredericksburg in Hooker's unfortunate Virginia campaign. We felt a genuine soldierly pride in such an association. We were now the comrades in arms of men whose business was fighting, and who attended to their business like men; and them we trusted to show us the way we were to follow. Our expectation that notwithstanding all our forced marching,

F

we were destined to return home without getting sight of the armed enemy was partially dissipated; and now that a live fighting man had got us in hand, there were few of us, it may well be supposed, who were any longer "spilin' for a fight." The veterans regarded our grey suits curiously, and advised us to exchange them for Uncle Sam's blue before we went into action; otherwise, we should most likely be taken for Grey Backs, (as the rebels were sometimes called by the Union soldiers from the color of their dress), and be shot by our comrades. This was not an over-pleasant suggestion; still, in the absence of present danger, we tried to " borrow no trouble".

General Meade, in his report of the Battle of Gettysburg, makes the following allusion to our arrival, though he erroneously makes Boonesboro' instead of Waynesboro' the place where we first joined him :—

" It is my duty as well as my pleasure to call attention to the earnest efforts at co-operation on the part of Major-General D. N. Couch, commanding the Department of the Susquehanna, and particularly to his advance of 4,000 men under Brigadier-General W. F. Smith, who joined me at Boonesboro' just prior to the withdrawal of the Confederate army."

We pitched our tents in a pleasant hill-side grove, where we rested the next day, employing our leisure in putting our arms in order. The morning report gave 519 officers and men as present and fit for the duty in the Twenty-Third regiment; the strongest muster the regiment could show during the campaign. Many of us got passes to go to Waynesboro' where, notwithstanding the rebels had, a few days before, seized all they could lay hands on, we found pretty much all we wanted; and having just come "out of the wilderness", we wanted pretty much everything that soldiers can use at once, or can carry away with them. The Little Antietam still kept us company, and bathing in its waters greatly refreshed our wearied limbs.

Friday, 10*th.*—Ordered out on a reconnoissance with the New York Seventy-First. The column moved out on the Waynesboro' and Greencastle pike, and took position on a bare hill some two or three miles east of Waynesboro'. Here we stacked arms and roasted in the sun all day; at night returned to camp.

Saturday, 11*th.*—Rested again, though we were on the *qui vive* all the afternoon for a forward movement, the following order having been promulgated :—

"Head-Quarters First Division, \
Department of the Susquehanna, \
Waynesboro', July 11th, 1863.

The Brigadier-General Commanding calls the attention of the command to the certainty of an early engagement with the enemy, and it is strictly enjoined upon Brigade, Regimental and Company commanders to attend at once to the condition of the arms and ammunition of the men under them.

No time is to be lost in putting the arms in perfect order and seeing that the boxes are filled with cartridges.

The rations on hand must be cooked and put in haversacks, so that no detention will ensue when the order to march is given; and also that the men may not suffer for food, when it is impossible for the supply trains to reach them.

By order of

Brig.-Gen. W. F. SMITH."

It was found that few or none of us had the full complement of forty rounds of ball cartridges in good order, our stock never having been replenished since we left Fort Washington. Our ammunition pouches being of insufficient capacity we had been obliged to carry a portion of the cartridges in our haversacks, which, in common with the clothes we wore, had been repeatedly soaked by the rain.

About the middle of the afternoon we heard distinct cannonading, which proved to proceed from a skirmish arising out of the movement of General Meade toward the front of the enemy's position at Williamsport. Reports were current, and credited, of another general battle on yesterday, in which Lee had been worsted, and it was expected that it would be renewed to-day. Thus we had on the whole a good prospect of being present, and having a share, in the enactment of another scene in the glorious drama. Toward sunset came marching orders. We proceeded in the direction of Hagerstown. Some two miles or more out the road crosses the Antietam, the bridge over which the rebels had destroyed. We waded the stream without wetting our trowsers, and marched our feet dry before coming to a halt for the night, some three or four miles further on. We were now on the soil of Maryland, the bridge over the Antietam being a little south of "Masonandicksun"; and we accordingly set up the air of "Dixie" with Yankee variations and a rousing chorus.

Just at dark we turned into a clover field and bivouacked noiselessly, spreading our rubber cloths and lying down, each man behind his piece, ready to seize arms instantly on an alarm. No fires were built, no loud talking allowed. It was like the crouching of a tiger making ready to spring upon its prey. These hints of the proximity of the enemy were quite enough to satisfy our curiosity on the subject, particularly as the Twenty-Third had the right of the line. Still we stretched ourselves for sleep without alarm, though not without emotion, and perhaps, anxiety. A few rods off, in a hollow of the field, a cloud of fog lay along the ground—its ominous grey just visible in the deepening twilight—and it was plainly creeping up to envelop us in its chilly arms. The night bade fair to be a foul one—to use a hibernicism—and none of us coveted the post of the picket in those black woods in front of us. But some one had to perform that trying duty; and it fell to the lot of Company "B" of the Twenty-Third to be detailed with others to the service, the command of the detachment being entrusted to Captain Goldthwait. The delicacy and danger of this service are well told in the words of the captain commanding:—

      Cavetown, Md., July 12th, 1863.

COLONEL:—

 In compliance with your orders I left the bivouac of the regiment on the Hagerstown road beyond Lietersburg last evening, and reported to General Knipe for picket duty. Upon filing into the road we found a company of the Seventy-First, N.Y., and a squad of the Third Pennsylvania Cavalry awaiting us. Reporting to the General we took the right of the Seventy-First, and with the cavalry in advance moved out on the Hagerstown road across a stone bridge to a point designated on the diagram by a haystack, at which point, by direction of the General, the reserve was stationed. After giving me instructions as to the direction in which he wished the line of pickets extended, and orders to hold the point to the latest possible moment, and under no circumstances to lose the bridge in our rear, the General returned to the brigade, and I proceeded to post the picket line.

The cavalry in the mean time had pushed forward on the road to hill (No. 1 on the diagram) when they encountered a vidette of the enemy's cavalry, which they drove from the position.

The hill being an excellent point for observation, a vidette of our cavalry was posted at that point. A chain of infantry pickets was thrown out on either flank towards the woods on our right and left, the sentinels for which were furnished in due proportion from my own and the company of the Seventy-First. The cavalry vidette reported that the rebels could be heard moving about all night.

At daylight we stood to arms, and the cavalry were sent out as far as the second hill, but found no enemy in sight.

I learned from a man living just beyond our line that the rebels in force, of all arms, had passed, the afternoon before (the 11th), in two columns, one keeping the road, and the other following the fields in a line parallel with the road. From this and other information obtained, I have no doubt that the main body of the rebels were last night in and around Hagerstown, which is about four miles from where our pickets were posted. At six o'clock this morning I was ordered to draw in the pickets and return to the column, which we found lying in the road where we rejoined it.

In closing this brief report, Colonel, I beg leave to say that while I never had a doubt as to the behavior of the Twenty-Third as a regiment, I was unprepared to meet with the cheerful obedience to orders which sent individuals into almost isolated positions where they had every reason to suppose that the enemy was within a few rods of them, and where the darkness was so intense as to limit the vision to a space of a few feet

Very respectfully,

C. E. GOLDTHWAIT,
Capt Co " B ", 23d Reg. N. G. S. N Y.,
Com'g Pickets."

Recalling to mind all the circumstances of the case, there is something in the thought of that night's bivouac which is awe-inspiring; — three or four thousand men massed in a field sleeping;

their stacked arms standing over them like sentinels; a thick fog encompassing them, and affording cover to an enemy to approach unseen; that enemy within easy striking distance, at bay, and watching doubtless for an opportunity to strike a sudden blow. The night passed quietly however, nothing being heard of the enemy, and we slept pretty well with the ghostly fog for our coverlet.

Sunday, 12th.— About six o'clock, after breakfasting very soberly and contentedly on hard tack and water, we got in motion again. A countermarch of a mile brought us to Lettersburg, a poor village of a dozen indifferent houses, through which we passed the evening before almost without noticing it. Here we turned off to the right, taking the Cavetown road. We crept along, continually halting, and reached Cavetown at noon, some seven miles south-east of Lettersburg, our path for the last mile being across fields and up hill to an extended plateau overlooking the village. Here, while resting, we were overtaken by a fierce thunder-storm. Six or eight miles in front of us to the eastward, South Mountain stood out in bold relief; and the peals of thunder reverberating against its sides made the valley ring again. The place takes its name from a natural cave near the spot where we were halted, and which afforded shelter to some of us from the shower. Here a cow, as wise as ourselves in this particular, had taken refuge, and kindly supplied us a few drops of milk. The art of extracting this nutritious liquid we learned at the outset of our campaign, and found the knowledge useful not unfrequently as we went along. Hard tack was no such delicious viand as made us despise the free gift of the cow. We found in the cave also what refreshed us almost as much—pure cold water. It was held in honey-comb cells or cups formed in the rock, twenty or more in number, holding three to six gallons each, the whole together forming an irregular shelf along one side of the cavern. There were dark passages and mysterious inner chambers, vaguely reported to be half a mile in extent, but we had no time to make further explorations. Before the shower ceased we were ordered to move, and proceeded down the face of the hill to the selected halting ground on the Hagerstown pike, a little out of the village. Here the column made bivouac, and guns were planted commanding the road to the front.

The rain continued to fall, and in such torrents as to inundate the camping ground. The air was filled with electricity, the crashing thunder reverberating almost incessantly for half an hour through the valley; and mournful to relate, some poor fellows of the Fifty-Sixth Regiment, N.Y., who had imprudently taken refuge under a tree, were struck by the electric fluid, and one of them killed.

The state of the ground compelled us to improvise dry beds, which we did by taking fence rails and laying them side by side on the ground. The idea of lying down to sleep on such a style of mattress was preposterous to most of us; still we could not deny that it had the first requisite of a bed, viz., dryness. Any one who has slept directly upon ploughed, stony ground, as was often our lot, knows how difficult it is to adjust the weary body to the crags and cañons of the surface — for the irregularities grow to be such before morning — and how the rest continues to be broken, night after night, until the flesh has become ferruginous, and the nerves indifferent to the welfare of the body, which no longer demands a nice adjustment of particulars, but finds sound sleep on a pile of big stones with the head resting on a stump. As we were most of us yet in our infancy as campaigners, we had not reached this perfection of indifference; and accordingly were delighted to find how nicely we could fit ourselves in among the rails.

Our sole reliance for rations appearing now to be upon the hard tack in our haversacks, eked out by an occasional loaf of bread, a jar of butter, apple sauce, or plum sauce which the company foragers were lucky enough to pick up, there was great temptation whenever we came to a halt to indulge in a little desultory foraging on private account; and as we were now in a farming country there was considerable of this done. But if the sight of a distant farm house, with the hope of chickens and cherry trees swimming before the mind, tempted any of us to indulge without leave in this agreeable recreation so long as to miss a roll-call, we had a vivid consciousness of sundry extra detail duties of police or guard awaiting us on our return. This gave a zest to the enjoyment of the stolen furlough, though it was not apt to be considered a severely "healthy" termination of an hour off duty. These penalties were a wiser disciplinary regimen than a rigid system of provost guards would have been, since it saved the strength of the regiment for the next day's march, and put the drudgeries of camp duty upon those who had fairly earned the right, and were also best able to perform them.

Before the afternoon had passed, however, our commissariat was amply provided for. Several fat steers were driven into camp, slaughtered and divided up among the hungry regiments; while the company cooks were not slow in doing their parts. Some of us had got by hook or by crook a cake of chocolate, and some a little coffee or tea, which gave rise to a good deal of lively cup and kettle boiling on private account, which kept the fires going briskly till dark.

The principal ingredient of some of the beverages which tasted so deliciously on that occasion, as well as some of the soups, etc., it may not be amiss to reveal, now that it is all past; though at the time it was judiciously kept a secret, doubtless. In a field near by there was a pretty brook half hidden among grass and bushes. The men of various regiments soon spied it out, and straightway it was lined with bipeds, of whom it is enough to say that they were travel-stained, who stood washing in it their persons and their clothes. Its course lay across the field to the road, where it was caught in a horse-trough. To this trough came file after file of men with great black kettles to be filled. The color of the water was such as to excite the indignant protest of every one who came there to draw, against the scores of animals in United States uniform who went above the trough to wash, instead of below. But it was of no avail;

the fringe of washers was constantly replenished by fresh comers, and the water was constantly drawn below; and there was made of it, no doubt, excellent soup, coffee, tea, chocolate, and whatever other delicious thing the regimental or private commissariat afforded. But lest some reader should be offended by this peep behind the scenes, it may be stated that there was another fountain whence some of the regiments drew,—a well at a neighboring farm-house which gave pure water, until it was pumped dry!

By this time General Meade with the bulk of his army was confronting the enemy, who had taken up "a strong position on the heights near the marsh which runs in advance of Williamsport". Lee had been busily engaged securing his retreat by rebuilding the pontoon bridge at Falling Waters which General French had partially destroyed, and was, no doubt, anxiously awaiting the subsidence of the Potomac to enable him to use the fords so as to escape suddenly under cover of the darkness.

Monday, 13th.—We were up bright and early, none the worse it is believed for the rough accommodations of the night; some of the most ailing, indeed, having had furloughs granted them till early morning, and having succeeded in finding more comfortable quarters in barns, or in the houses of the village. The rain having ceased we got our things well dried before the fires, and broke camp at 6½ o'clock, setting out in the direction of Boonesboro'. The morning was comfortable, the sun was obscured, and a cool breeze was blowing. Before noon we came to a halt in a wood, having made some six miles. Here a pleasant sight greeted Company A, of the Twenty-Third. Foragers had been sent out in advance when we broke camp, one or two for each company it was said. One of these now made his appearance, having in company a poor farmer whom he had found up in the mountains. He was dressed in jean blouse and overalls, wore a slouched hat, and sat astride a small imitation of a horse, which bore also two well-filled bags slung across his back, before and behind the rider. These bags disgorged lima beans, onions, radishes, a pile of fresh bread and a crock of butter; none of which, it may well be believed, were wasted. On this halt we were treated to our usual daily ration of shower — the only ration we received regularly. It rained for several hours, wetting us enough to make us miserable. Early in the afternoon we got started again, much to our relief.

As we were now entered upon the last week of

our term of service, and as there did not appear to us to be any immediate prospect of further fighting—at least of fighting in which we should be engaged—we had been thinking all day that our faces were at length set toward home, and that Boonesboro' was to be the next stage of our journey; then some point between Boonesboro' and Frederick; then Frederick, where we should find railroad transportation direct for Baltimore, Philadelphia and New York. This was a pretty fancy, and we discussed it with great vivacity. It beguiled the march and helped us amazingly over the abominable roads and through the more abominable rain. There was but little singing, however, "Homeward Bound" being as yet far from *fait accompli*. Besides, we had not been in singing mood, as a general thing, these many days—marching along usually with a quiet, dogged, philosophic endurance of discomfort.

But these visions of home with which we had filled one another's hearts we knew hardly deserved any better name than day-dreams; for though we were marching toward home, we were also marching toward the enemy, General Meade being at that very moment, though happily for our dreams we knew it not, feeling the enemy and preparing for a vigorous attack upon him on the morrow; in which prospective event we were doubtless looked to as a portion of the reserve force. This tended to sober the exuberance of our hopes. It was interesting to watch in the spirit of the men the play of this struggle between hope and fear. We had marched but a mile or two from the wood when we made another halt in a field by the road. In a certain part of the line a little company fell together worthy of brief mention. One, a singer, had spread out his rubber cloth upon the wet ground, and was reclining upon it. Eight others had joined him, also singers, sitting down on the edges of the cloth; and they were singing together. A row of listeners sat perched on a rail fence five or six feet in front of them, and others were ranged around in various picturesque situations and attitudes. These swelled the choruses and joined in the melody according to their skill and knowledge. And what did they sing? " Gideon's Band"? "Hail Columbia"? "Kingdom Coming"? or any of those songs with which we were wont days before to greet the larks and the freshly risen sun when resuming the march after an uncomfortable bivouac? No, nothing of the sort. But in soft low tones they warbled the most plaintive songs. Because of our hope, we counted over and over again the remaining days of wandering allotted to us by the terms of our enlistment, and beguiled one another with scenes of home revisited. But because there was fear and uncertainty mingled with our hope, we thought of that home tenderly, and were in no mood of exultation in our singing. Those who remember that little chance way-side festival will have no difficulty of recognising the spirit which animated it in the following melodies, which were always great favorites with us when we were in a plaintive mood: —

> Why am I so weak and weary?
>   See how faint my heated breath!
> All around to me seems darkness;
>   Tell me, comrades, is this death?
> Ah! how well I know your answer;
>   To my fate I'll meekly bow,
> If you'll only tell me truly,
>   Who will care for mother now?
>
> CHORUS: Soon with angels I'll be marching,
>   With bright laurels on my brow;
>   I have for my Country fallen,
>   Who will care for mother now?
>
> Who will comfort her in sorrow?
>   Who will dry the falling tear?
> Gently smooth her wrinkled forehead?
>   Who will whisper words of cheer?
> Even now I think I see her
>   Kneeling, praying for me! How
> Can I leave her in her anguish?
>   Who will care for mother now?

> Let this knapsack be my pillow,
> And my mantle be the sky;
> Hasten, comrades, to the battle!
> I will like a soldier die.
> Soon with angels I'll be marching,
> With bright laurels on my brow:
> I have for my Country fallen.
> Who will care for mother now?

The following is inserted, like the rest not on account of any intrinsic merit it may be thought to have, nor indeed on account of any sympathy for the slave which it might have been employed to express—though there was probably no lack of that—but because it illustrates, in words and music, a certain sentimental vein of feeling which found frequent utterance, not very soldier-like it must be confessed, nor indulged when serious work was before us to do, but quite natural to us now that we had caught half-visions of home, albeit in the intervening sky there were omens of doubtful import.

> There's a low green valley on the old Kentucky shore:
> There I've whiled many happy hours away,
> A sitting and a singing by the little cottage door
> Where lived my darling Nelly Gray.
>
> CHORUS.
>
> Oh, my poor Nelly Gray, they have taken you away,
> And I'll never see my darling any more,
> I'm sitting by the river and I'm weeping all the day,
> For you've gone from the old Kentucky shore.

One night I went to see her, but she's gone, the neighbours say,
    The white man has bound her with his chain ;
They have taken her to Georgia for to wear her life away,
    As she toils in the cotton and the cane.

My eyes are getting blinded and I cannot see my way,
    Hark ! there's somebody knocking at the door ;
Oh, I hear the angels calling and I see my Nelly Gray:
    Farewell to the old Kentucky shore.

CHORUS.

Oh, my Nelly Gray, up in heaven there they say
    They will never take you from me any more ;
I'm a coming, coming, coming as the angels clear the way ;
    Farewell to the old Kentucky shore.

We had dropped down on the ground with our harness on expecting to hear the "Fall in" at any moment; but it was in the edge of the evening before we were summoned to resume the march. A mile or two further brought us to camping ground in a rough, ploughed field within about a mile of Boonesboro'. As dark was fast coming on all hands set to, on breaking ranks, and brought rails for fires and bedding ! It was astonishing to watch the effect of this instantaneous assault upon the fences. They melted away before the eyes very much like a flake of snow does on the warm ground; it disappears while you are looking at it, almost before you have half realized that it is going ! The pots were on in a trice, and by the time we had tents pitched we were saluted with the " Fall in" for soup. The bustle over, we had time to look about us, and then for the first some of us saw what caused a sudden change to come o'er the spirit of our dreams. It was now dark. In the distance in fr8nt and on the right appeared the gleam of camp fires; and on the left far up in mid-air a bright light was blazing which we knew at once to be a beacon on South Mountain, many miles distant, though it was too dark to see even the outline of the range. That spot of fire, hanging aloft there in the pitchy darkness like a great meteor, had in it somewhat of portentous awe to us. It seemed the eye of a Cyclops watching the foe. Our imaginations had not yet taken in the scope of a vast army, nor the stupendous movements of a great battle like Gettysburg. The apparition of extended camp fires and a great beacon afar off came suddenly upon us as out of the very darkness. We had been beguiling the day with visions of home, and cheating ourselves with the dream that we were even then homeward bound; and now to have thrust upon us without warning the spectral lights of a great army, and to be set down in the midst of them was startling. But the surprise over, the sight was exhilarating. Close about us lay encamped the several regiments comprising our column, where a hundred fires were blazing. Around them figures were moving like Indians, whose faces the flames lit up with ghastly distinctness. The neighboring wood was made visible and gloomy at once by the fires under the trees, the foliage' reflecting the light dismally. Elsewhere all was in darkness, and we lay down to sleep wondering what the morrow would bring forth. Frederick City and home were forgotten, and the thoughts that now possessed us were of marching and counter-marching, of lines of battle, of reserves, of battery supports, and the like.

General Meade had spent the day in making "reconnoissances of the enemy's position and preparations for an attack" on the morrow; and General Lee in completing his preparations to withdraw to the south side of the river, which he expected to accomplish during the night; but "owing to the condition of the roads the troops (rebel) did not reach the bridge until after daylight on the 14th, and the crossing was not completed until 1 P.M., when the bridge was removed."

Tuesday, 14th.—The morning dawned but brought to us no appearance of impending battle; and probably in the event of a battle, the first intimation we should have had of it would have been the distant roar of artillery. And this we heard about noon—doubtless the attack of General Kilpatrick's cavalry upon the enemy's rear-guard at Falling Waters, which resulted in the fall of the rebel general Pettigrew, who was in command of the rear-guard, and the capture of two pieces of artillery and fifteen hundred prisoners.

About this time we were ordered under arms again. By slow, short stages we crept across the fields to the Boonesboro' and Hagerstown pike, which we followed toward the latter city two miles. We passed a spot where there had lately been a great camp—the fences all gone, the fields one vast common and trampled foul, and the air loaded with stench from putrid carcasses. There were some troops still remaining, also a park of army wagons, hundreds in number, and a large drove of fat cattle. When we thought of our starved commissariat, this sight made us inclined to envy the lot of the soldiers of the Grand Army.

We halted in a field, through which runs a considerable stream called Beaver Creek, a tributary of the Antietam, within thirty rods of where there had been a cavalry fight a few days before. It was stated that our men buried some bodies of rebel soldiers that afternoon. Toward evening news came that put an entirely new face upon affairs.

IV.

HOMEWARD BOUND.

By late Baltimore papers we learned of the great riot in New York; that Chief of Police Kennedy had been killed; that the militia, called out in defence of the city, had been disarmed by the mob; that the office of the *Tribune* had been torn down; besides a great many other things to match. This created somewhat of a stir in camp as may be imagined. It was not pleasant to think of our firesides and our property and those of our fellow-citizens exposed to the mercies of mob law, and we, to whom the city was accustomed to look for protection against such violence, unable to defend them. Under purely patriotic impulses we had rushed to the rescue of an invaded sister state to do the little we could toward destroying the great enemy of our country; and now to be assailed by this dastardly fire in the rear made us turn with even a sharper vengeance against the insurgents at home than we felt towards the armed hosts which confronted us. Nor had home-sickness anything to do with this feeling. It is true, the idea which was involved, of going home, modified secondarily the tone of our spirits and made us jubilant, without, however, diluting our eagerness to be seen marching up Broadway with firm step to the rescue of our own dishonored metropolis. During the remainder of the afternoon this news was the staple of our talk, and we chafed to be off at once. Some of the regiments appeared to be in possession of specially gladdening news; for they filled the camp with cheering and hilarious singing. This spirit was contagious, and a remarkably buoyant feeling quickly overspread the whole encampment. But

" The best laid schemes o' mice an' men
  Gang aft a-gley ; "

and like sensible men we put not our trust in princes. Accordingly the opportunity of getting a fresh supply of delicacies being presented, we availed ourselves of it precisely as if we understood that we were to resume pursuit of the enemy on

G

the morrow. Boonsboro' was only some four miles distant, and men were detailed to go thither, and get what they could, though the supply of store goods was extremely problematical since the rebels, with maws more insatiable than ours, had occupied the place but a few days previously, and must have lovingly visited the shops. Commissions were given for the purchase of all sorts of things — things to eat, things to drink, things to wear, things to cook in.

Toward evening the chaplain held a prayer-meeting under a spreading tree. These meetings which had been so acceptable to us while we lay at Fort Washington were now grown almost totally into disuse. During the severities of the campaign it would have been a forlorn task to meet together either at the close or the beginning of the day for even the solemn services of religion. Our strength was always near the point of exhaustion, and it was doubtless the feeling of all who thought about it that we were serving our Maker better by husbanding all our physical powers for use against the armed enemies of law and order, of republican government and personal liberty, of society and religion, than we should be by spending in public prayer, singing and exhortation the precious hours that would otherwise be given to rest. In ;,e silence of the heart with brief and often painful ejaculations, and in the nakedness of truth, which no public ceremony can so much as imitate, did worship go up to heaven from every devout heart among us, during those days and nights of suffering. The sharpness of our tribulation was our best chaplain, pointing to us the way and helping our feeble wills to walk in it. We needed then no other.

Under the inspiration of the morrow's hope there was a great demonstration of joy in camp. Throughout the evening the air was filled with cadences of happy song and with uproarious shouting; and all felt, as we stretched ourselves in our tents for sleep that the morning would bring us assurances that we were homeward bound.

Wednesday, 15th.—Morning dawned through a dripping atmosphere as usual. We piled together the half burnt fagots, and rejoiced with the leaping flames in the expectancy of receiving immediate marching orders. We cooked coffee and soup, the partaking of which was not observed to result injuriously, strange as it may seem, and dried our tents, blankets, overcoats, etc. But no marching orders came. Nobody knew what was going to be done. We were packed and all ready for the final word, but that final word seemed fatefully to linger. It was a period of anxious suspense. We were yet a part of the Army of the Potomac, and in the very midst of it. General Meade's headquarters were near. The enemy we supposed were still at bay in the mountains this side the river. It was evident that now was the auspicious moment to strike at him with all the might of the Grand Army. At that moment Madam Rumor whispered that Lee had eluded us and slipped across the Potomac! If this were true the golden opportunity was again lost, and the campaign at an end. Perhaps the wish was father to the thought, but we could not believe we were to be marched off into Virginia in pursuit. And yet if it were intended to send us home what meant this delay, during which the cool hours were fast slipping by. The camp grew moody. Some threw themselves upon the ground in drowsy unrest; some sat down against the shocks of wheat with which the field was strewn and read the newspapers drearily, or with affected indifference went napping; some wandered off to the stream, but quickly returned under an irrepressible nervous anxiety. At length a feeling not unlike disgust seemed taking possession of us, when shortly before eight o'clock word came! It swept through the camp like an electric current. "Fall in!" shouted the orderly. "Fall in!" shouted back the men. "Fall in! Fall in!" echoed from every quarter. We jumped into our harness, quickly got into line, and at eight o'clock were on the road with our faces toward Frederick, this time homeward bound in sober verity.

With this change in our affairs our relations to the Army of the Potomac terminated, and we were turned over to our own militia officers by the following order:

Head-Quarters, First Division,
Department of the Susquehanna.

Special Order No.—   July 15th, 1853.

Brigadier-General John Ewen will take command of all the New York troops in this Division, and proceed with them to Frederick, Maryland, at which point transportation will be furnished them to New York City. In parting with them the General Commanding must express his admiration of the courage and fortitude with which they have stood the toils and privations of their late marches.

By order of
Brigadier-General W. F. SMITH.
PRESTON F. WEST, A. A. A. G.

The tribute to our fidelity paid us in this hastily penned order will lose nothing of its value when read in connection with the ungenerous slur upon our trustworthiness contained in the paragraph, before alluded to, of General Halleck's Review.

Nor was General Meade unmindful of what was due to us, as witness the following:

Head-Quarters, Army of the Potomac,
July 15, 1863.

Special Order, No. 190.

The troops comprising the command of Brigadier-General W. F. Smith are released from further service with the Army of the Potomac, and will be reported back to General Couch for instructions. The Major-General Commanding thanks Brigadier-General W. F. Smith and his troops for the zeal and promptitude which, amid no little privations, have marked their efforts to render this army all the assistance in their power.   *   *   *   *   *   *

By command of

Major-General MEADE.

S. WILLIAMS, A. A. G.

On the eve of our departure homeward there were signs in camp of a mail having arrived with news from home. Beside the usual precious gift of letters there flamed out from the persons of many of the fellows—especially the younger men, quite an assortment of patriotic and other symbols. One flaunted a pretty tri-color, jauntily pinned on the breast of his coat, evidently just extracted from a dainty looking letter which he was reading. Ah, I fear me, the delicate thought of a sweetheart thrilled in that bosom, while coarser eyes only saw fluttering on the outside a tiny badge of red, white and blue. Another sported a miniature flag in the form of a pin; and other devices there were according to the fancy of the fair correspondent. Did these highly favored fellows know, I wonder, through what tribulations these precious messages had passed to reach their hands? All knew how, owing to our constant and rapid marches, and the impracticable condition of the roads, we had been deprived, ever since we left Harrisburg, of all means of communicating with home except as accident provided. The chaplain of the Twenty-Third interested himself in forwarding our letters whenever there seemed to be a reasonable chance of getting them through. But we were all indebted more than once to the energy and kindness of a gentleman of New-York, not connected with any of the regiments, for tidings from home and for the opportunity of sending return letters.[*]

---

[*] As this gentleman[†] in making his way to join us went over much the same ground that we did, his observations are interesting as showing how things looked in our wake. His adventures, moreover, are full of entertainment as well on account of their novelty and freshness as for the remarkable energy displayed in overcoming obstacles that would have appalled most men.

On the fifth of July he obtained after great difficulty a pass to

---

[†] JOHN H. TRIPLER, Esq.

Our march being now directed homeward it may be imagined that our step was light, and our hearts also. The woods again resounded to joyous singing which broke from all parts of the line.

---

cross the bridge at Harrisburg; and having reached Carlisle the same afternoon by the cars, set out with one or two others on foot to overtake the column. At Papertown they halted for the night at a deserted house, where they found "some soldiers sitting around on the floor eating bread and molasses by the light of a dilapidated tallow candle." Next morning they entered upon the mountain road leading to Laurel Forge, which they found still nearly impassable. In the words of the narrator, "It was nothing but mud, mud, of the worst kind. Thus we travelled for many weary miles till we came to where a number of the Thirty-Seventh Regiment had been encamped with their teams. The road grew worse as we proceeded. We began now to pass a good many stragglers and wagons, some of them stuck in the mud, the soldiers with ropes assisting the horses to get through the well-nigh impassable mire. We came to a wagon that had broken down, belonging to the Thirty-Seventh, and found in it a barrel of hard-tack from which we filled our handkerchiefs and ate along the way, soaking it in the brooks to make it easier for our molars. We were told for our encouragement that the further we proceeded the less chance we would have of getting anything to eat; and we found it so. We had not gone far before we came across some hungry soldiers who gladly took some of our crackers." Our travellers were lucky enough to find a roof to sleep under that night but had to go to bed supperless.

"On Tuesday morning we proceeded on our way hungry, being unable to procure breakfast; the poor man who gave us lodging having been robbed by the rebels, who had not left him enough for his own family. The roads being here lined with cherry trees, we followed the example of the soldiers and satisfied the cravings of appetite with this refreshing fruit. * * We at length reached Cashtown, where we found the main body of our New York and Brooklyn regiments encamped. * * We found a great many had letters to send home, which we volunteered to carry, there

During the wearisome and forlorn marches of the last fortnight silence had for the most part fitlier expressed our emotions; or, if we sang, the melodies were pensive and often sad. But now all was

---

being no regular way of sending them. They soon had us pretty heavily laden; so with a soldier's haversack over each shoulder we marched along with the column when it moved."

At Altodale our friend "after getting all the letters for New York" took final leave of us, and started alone to return. Thinking he might be molested on the road at night—for he meant to travel the greatest number of hours that his strength would permit—he armed himself with a pass from headquarters. "I left," he continues, "about half-past eight o'clock in the evening intending to go as far as possible before resting. But the night being dark, there being some danger of falling into the hands of the rebels, and the few straggling soldiers with whom I was in company not being willing to proceed further, I concluded to halt at the first house I came to. I was up in the night several times from anxiety of mind, and about two o'clock in the morning, the moon having risen sufficiently to make the road visible, I roused the farmer, settled my bill and made my exit. No sooner had I got into the road than I was peremptorily ordered to 'halt!' The summons proved to proceed from a picket of the Thirteenth Regiment, who hailed a comrade and carefully inspected my pass by the light of a lantern. This proving satisfactory I proceeded on my lonely journey. A heavy rain soon set in which wet me through, adding to my discomfort." During the hours of darkness he stumbled upon various suspicious parties whom, being off their guard, having crawled under shelter from the rain, and being perhaps asleep, he managed to avoid, fearing they were rebels. One of these parties he learned to be Independent Pennsylvania Pickets *guarding the road!* "After a tedious journey," he goes on to say, "I arrived at Fayetteville about five o'clook in the morning. Arousing one of the storekeepers, I got all the information I could regarding my journey, and procured breakfast. The storm gave no signs of abating, but I was determined to proceed notwithstanding the roads were fast becoming

G*

changed. We saw that our painful trials were rapidly drawing to a close, and it is only the truth to say that we rejoiced with exceeding joy.

The distance to Frederick where we expected

---

impassable I found the bridges washed away, and the roads overflowed; but I soon got used to wading up to my waist in water. I at length came to a stream which I found unfordable, the bridge having been destroyed by the rebels. I was told that this was the heaviest freshet that had ever been known in those parts. Having engaged a boy to pilot me across the stream, I gave him charge of one of my mail bags and cautiously followed him. We found a temporary structure crossing the stream, along which we picked our way. But when we had got about half across the whole structure gave way and we found ourselves floundering in the water. After desperate exertions we managed to reach the shore, and I proceeded on my journey. I at length came to a rail-road, or the remains of one. The rebels had torn it up, burnt the sleepers, and twisted the rails into every imaginable shape.   *   *   I reached Shippensburg in time to learn that there was no train till next morning. Although tired out I concluded to push on to Carlisle in hopes of catching a soldier's train at that place.   *   *   About six o'clock in the evening I arrived at a small village where I got supper. About seven o'clock I started again for a night's tramp, not being able to obtain any conveyance. I walked on till dark by a very circuitous and muddy road, being at times bewildered; till finally my route seemed to lie along a large stream of water. I was now becoming scarcely able to stand from so many hours' severe walking, occasionally stumbled headlong, in danger constantly of walking into the river. It became very dark, and the mist rising from the river made the road and water all look alike, and I had to feel my way along step by step.   *   *   A few miles further I heard the welcome sound of a locomotive which served as a guide to the Newville Depot, where I arrived about half-past eleven o'clock.*

---

* Our self-forgetting traveller omits to give the distances of the remarkable journey he is pursuing. On the morning of the 6th he left Papertown; on the evening of the 7th he parted with the troops at Altodale; and now a little

to get railroad transportation we understood to be
upwards of twenty miles, a two days' march at the
rate at which we had hitherto moved. But the
road was good, though being macadamised it was

" Learning that no train would start for Harrisburg till towards
morning, I took a room and went to bed. About one o'clock I
heard a locomotive whistle, and hastily dressing, hurried down only
to find it was a soldiers' train going to Shippensburg; *but concluded
not to go to bed again for fear I should miss the earliest train eastward* (!)
I spent the balance of the night in an engine room of the station
drying my clothes and the letters, and took a train in the morning
for Harrisburg, and thence to New York, where I arrived about ten
o'clock at night." On that night he sorted the Brooklyn letters, and
personally delivered most of them early on the following morning!

In a second expedition undertaken for a similar benevolent object,
this resolute and indefatigable traveller recounts some amusing
tribulations which he suffered in order to secure safe transit for a
" large trunk filled with tobacco for the boys"—worth its weight in
gold to the tobacco-famished regiments. Among other forwarding
agents whose services he appropriated was one " Nat Wolf, who
had recently been employed by the rebels in conveying dead
soldiers", having been impressed by them when they passed by his
manor. Nat showed what he called his " Pass", written on a piece
of brown paper and signed by the rebel general Heath, which ex-
empted him from further impressment into the rebel service on
account of his "extreme poverty, and the unfitness of his horse and
wagon to be of any further service" to their army! When it is considered what the exigencies of the rebel service are in the best of
times, some idea may be formed of the prospective perils of the
journey about to be undertaken by our traveller! But " Nat

---

before midnight of the 8th he is at Newville — having walked a distance which
cannot be much short of NINETY MILES in some *sixty-five hours*; carrying for
more than one-half of the distance about *one thousand letters*, whose weight
could not have been less than THIRTY POUNDS — all this through drenching
rains and over horrible roads ; and fording or swimming streams whose
bridges had been swept away by the flood !

hard for the feet, and we made but few rests. During the forenoon we caught sight of an army wagon train ahead of us in the distance, the white canvas covers dotting the road for miles like flecks of wool. The solidity of these wagons, which occasionally passed us singly, and the excellent condition of the teams excited our admiration, they contrasted so strikingly with our own. Each was drawn by four to six mules, fat, sleek, natty-looking creatures, which are taught to obey the voice instead of the rein like oxen. Though from what has been said of the staple of the soldiers' vocabulary—and it may be imagined the teamsters were not a whit behind—this use cannot be commended on moral grounds for the sake of either man or beast.

At noon we halted an hour or more in a deep, wide dell by the roadside, where we ate our rations of hard-tack which we carried in haversacks, rested a little, rambled a little, foraged a little; cooked

---

Wolf"—his wagon "tied together with ropes"—brought his rare freight through in safety, not to speak of dispatch. Collecting another "large mail". Mr. T. at once set out for home again, and delivered his precious charge at an early day, notwithstanding an alarming attack of sickness which overtook him at Frederick, Md.

Such zeal in the voluntary service of the regiments, and such extraordinary exertions to relieve at the earliest possible moment the anxieties of thousands of hearts for whom he had most precious messages, is deserving of more than this passing recognition."

coffee, chocolate or tea; partook together of delicate bits which some had contrived to pick up; bathed our feet in a brook which threaded the dell; and in one way or another refreshed ourselves for a speedy resumption of the march.

The day throughout was favorable for a long march, the sun being somewhat obscured by clouds and the heat not excessive. The column kept well together, and it was a magnificent spectacle to watch the long line winding over the hills and through the hollows in the far distance. On reaching the crest of Catoctin mountain a sudden turn of the road unrolled all at once before us a superb panorama of the valley of the Monocacy and a vast spread of adjacent country, in the midst of which we could just distinguish afar off the spires of a city which we supposed to be Frederick. A little further on we beheld the city completely revealed before us in the beauty of a most quiet landscape. Our day's march, it was now evident, was not to terminate short of this place, and we were not sorry; for we expected to find transportation awaiting us there, and that we should be hurried on to New-York without an hour's delay.

It was amusing to observe the disposition among the men to collect souvenirs of the campaign, from the rusty iron button which a paroled rebel prisoner might be induced to cut from his coat, to a dog led by a string tied round his neck. In the dog line nothing appeared to be amiss. From a poodle pup to a raw-boned mongrel, whatever sort came along was sure to be gobbled up as if it had been a creature of superbest breed. It was not the value of the thing, but the association, that made it precious. The fancy however was short-lived. Perhaps the long march did not agree with the dogs; or their new proprietors grew weary of facing the storm of laughter which greeted them every little while when extricating their yelping charges from between their own or their comrades' legs among which they were forever getting tangled. Whatever the reason, the dogs disappeared, there being only one poor, limp, fagged-out mongrel left, according to the writer's observation, to enter with the stately column the city of Frederick. It is not impossible that some might have turned up in the shape of soup or stew, had our commissariat been subsequently in so suffering a condition as on some days and nights we had passed. At such times dog or cat or mule meat, well stewed, would have been accepted with enthusiasm and voted an immense success.

We entered Frederick toward the close of the day, and halted there for a couple of hours or more.

The shops were instantly besieged for eatables and drinkables of every description, but could do little toward supplying the ravenous demand. At dark we buckled on our harness again, having three miles yet between us and Monocacy Junction, where we were to take cars. As we neared the Junction the screaming and snorting of locomotives greeted our ears, and pleasanter sounds could hardly be imagined. The idea of a train of cars flying across the country had haunted us in many and many a toilsome march; and now to know that such was to bear us over the distance that yet intervened between us and our homes, and to hear its shrill greeting, and to catch sight of its glaring Cyclops-eye, all this was indeed exhilarant.

This last three miles was to some of us, probably to all, by far the severest part of the march; much severer than it would have been had the rest at Frederick been shorter. The day's performance was certainly a great feat, only exceeded in severity by our Fourth of July's march from Carlisle to Laurel Forge through a sea of mud. The distance from Beaver Creek to Frederick is something like twenty-two miles. We moved with equipments complete, even cartridge pouches filled. What kept us up was the near prospect of home which loomed glittering before our eyes, the knowledge that this was to be our last march, and a belief that a great emergency existed in New York requiring our immediate presence. But even under the stimulus of these inspiring motives it is remarkable that we kept up at all. One poor fellow, a member of the Fifty-Sixth, N.Y., had no sooner reached camp than his o'erwrought powers gave way, and he died in half an hour. He had the appearance of a hardy workingman. Strange that Death, for that day's fatigue, should have passed by men unused to severe toil, and lain his strong hand on one of sinewy frame.

The place of encampment was a piece of woods near the rail-road. The ground was somewhat damp and the air heavy with mist; but too fagged out to pitch tents, we spread our rubber blankets and dropped upon them. Moreover we did not suppose we were to rest there during the whole night, but expected to be called up soon to take the cars. In that bivouac, our bodies overheated and their nervous energy exhausted, there was peril, much greater peril than many of us thought of; but the night passed quietly and uneventfully.

Friday 17*th*.— The hours of Friday melted away one by one without bringing any intimation of a further movement. But a little after midnight following we were ordered into line to take the cars for Baltimore. It soon began to rain, and so continued till dawn ; during all which time we remained under arms on the road, waiting, and got thoroughly wet again. At dawn the Twenty-Third and Fifty-Sixth were packed aboard a train of thirty cars similar to those which transported us from Philadelphia to Harrisburg at the outset of our campaign, and which we had thought so wretched. Some of them were provided with three or four rough pine boards for seats, and the rest with nothing whatever. But now our plane of view was shifted greatly ; and the thought that our long marches, our exhausting fasts, our comfortless bivouacs were all ended, was so ravishing that we regarded the car as an asylum from misery.

We reached Baltimore about 4 p. m., where we got refreshments, and expected to take cars for Philadelphia at once, transportation having been secured for the Twenty-Third by its officers. The brigade, however, was ordered to proceed together *via* Harrisburg; and we accordingly marched across the city some two miles to the Harrisburg depot where we embarked about midnight on a train similar in style to that which had brought us from Frederick. Our progress was very slow, owing probably to interruptions on the road, the rebels having burnt the bridges and torn up and twisted the rails. Repairs were by this time nearly completed, though several structures we crossed were considered very unsafe for the passage of trains.

Saturday, 18*th*.—We spent the day for the most part on the car-tops which afforded a charming panorama of the pretty country we were traversing. The train being more than one half the time at a stand-still, some of us had the enterprise to build fires on the road and cook coffee; some hunted for berries; some ran off, at no small risk, to a neighboring farm-house for bread and butter, milk, cakes, pies, etc.; some whiled the time away with playing checkers, the squares being scratched on the tin roofs of the cars and small flakes of stones being used for pieces. At York we found awaiting our arrival a crowd of small venders of cakes, pies, etc., who brought their commodities eagerly to us, which we as eagerly purchased at outrageous prices.

Between York and Harrisburg we had a narrow escape of an an appalling calamity. A new bridge over a considerable confluent of the Susquehanna gave way under a freight and cattle train only a few hours before we reached the spot—the whole now presenting a frightful spectacle of wreck. We crossed the stream—some by a light pontoon bridge, and some clambering over the broken timbers and wrecked cars, and took a train on the other side which brought us safely to Harrisburg by dark. Here we were threatened with another delay, which was prevented, as we understood, by the resolution of our regimental officers. After partaking of lunch freely furnished at the soldiers' dining hall, we proceeded without change of cars toward home. Our berths for the night were somewhat promiscuously dovetailed together, not unlike a box of sardines. But notwithstanding an occasional kick in the face, or the racy smell of an old shoe not far removed from the detective organ, or other like reminders of our situation, we slept and were refreshed.

Sunday, 10th.—At Easton, Pa., we were met by a great concourse of people loaded down with food for us. It was morning church time; but they had heard of our coming, and that we had but little to eat, and here, behold, was an earnest of their Christianity. It was certainly a very beautiful spectacle :—men with piled up wagon loads of cooked meats, bread, cakes, etc., driving alongside the car doors and dispensing the viands with lavish hand; ladies toiling along under heavy baskets to the nearest who appeared to be yet unprovided for; nothing for money, all for charity. It may be guessed the stillness of that Sabbath air was broken by many a ringing cheer for those good Samaritans of Easton. The train stopped long enough to give us a chance to prink up a little; and one fellow had the hardihood to go off and get shaved. The shout of derision which greeted this youth when he showed himself was only equalled by the laughter with which we saluted the first man we saw carrying an umbrella!

At 3 P. M., we reached Elizabethport where we embarked in a steamer which was in waiting. Landed at the Battery and proceeded directly to the Armory where we were dismissed.

In the foregoing narrative I have not attempted to conceal or underrate our eagerness to get home. It is a feeling common to all soldiers when their term of service is drawing toward its close, and distant be the day when camp-life shall have such attractions for the American citizen as to make him indifferent to it. But now that our desire to see the familiar faces and renew the associations of our daily life was fulfilled, we felt a willingness to respond again to a similar call upon our patriotism, even though it were certain that similar sufferings were in store for us. The service we had rendered the government we knew to be honorable and valuable, and we rejoiced in having so rendered it as not to be ashamed to keep its memory green. And thereunto I would cherish every memento. The knapsack and haversack, torn, musty and rusty; the battered canteen; the belt and cartridge pouch; the woolen and rubber blankets, most indispensable of equipments;— these shall not be thrown aside among the rubbish, but cherished with an ever-growing affection. Nor let me forget my shelter tent. Ah that painful roll! with which I toiled, day after day, over the worst roads, enduring the tormenting burden for the sake of the rosy hope that at the end of the march it would repay me and perhaps some wretched comrade beside, by its warm protection; and not having despairingly thrown it away in those mountains of our sorrow I do now and shall henceforth cherish it as among sacred recollections. Set up in some quiet retreat of my garden, it may in after years serve to keep alive the waning fires of patriotism, as beneath it will be rehearsed the story of Gettysburg, never to be forgotten while the love of glorious deeds remains among men, with that episode of the Great Battle which the New York Militia enacted, insignificant only when compared with the grandeur of the main story.

APPENDIX.

RESUMÈ OF THE CAMPAIGN.

Tuesday, June 16th, 1863.—23d Reg. received marching orders.
Wednesday, 17th —Ready; waiting for transportation.
Thursday, 18th.—Embarked early in the day. Weather pleasant.
Friday, 19th.—Arrived, A.M., at Harrisburg, reporting to Major-General Couch; and P. M. at Bridgeport Heights. Afternoon and night stormy. Marched 5 miles.
Saturday, 20th.—Details at work in trenches. Guard duty on ramparts. Day cloudy and heavy rain throughout night.
Sunday, 21st.—Work of yesterday resumed. New camping ground laid out. Cloudy but no rain.
Monday, 22d.—Captain Farnham, Company C, 23d Regiment, appointed Acting Major of the regiment. 448 officers and men present for duty.
Tuesday, 23d.—Brig.-Gen. William Hall assumed command of all the troops in and about the fort. Col. William Everdell, jr., placed temporarily in command of the Eleventh Brigade, now consisting of 23d, 52d, and 56th Regiments. A squad of the 23d, twenty-two in number, arrived from Brooklyn.
Wednesday, 24th.—Usual routine of garrison duty.
Thursday, 25th.—Brig.-Gen. Jesse C. Smith arrived and took command of Eleventh Brigade, now comprising 1,124 officers and men. Last four days for the most part warm and pleasant, though heavy fogs prevalent night and morning.
Friday, 26th.—Left with two days' cooked provisions on tour of picket duty, to relieve 37th N.Y., Col. Roome. Rained in torrents. Detachments posted on the various roads, from one to three miles out. All quiet during the night.
Saturday, 27th.—Pickets moved forward to Shiremanstown. Toward evening the advance of 8th and 71st N.Y., who had been reconnoitering at the front since the 30th, appeared. Reported the enemy slowly advancing. Being relieved, returned, reaching the fort about midnight. Day lowering, little rain.
Sunday 28th.—Enemy constantly reported moving on our works. Garrison under arms throughout day and night. Glacis and space beyond cleared of trees and standing grain. Each company assigned its position at the breastworks. Day filled with alarms but passed without anything more serious. Guards doubled for the night. Cloudy and comfortable, but no rain.
Monday, 29th.—On the *qui vive*. Large detail from 23d for provost duty at the wagon bridge over the Susquehanna. Volunteer picket force went out composed of detachments from 8th, 56th and 23d, under command of Lieut.-Col. Elwell, 23d. Pickets shelled, but suffered no loss. Captured a rebel. Weather unsettled.

Tuesday, 30*th.*—Still on the alert. 22d and 37th N.Y. ordered out to reconnoiter. Expecting to return in course of the day left everything behind except arms and ammunition, and thus passed through rest of campaign! They moved along the Carlisle road to "Sporting Hill" where had a skirmish, in which lost three officers and four men wounded. A spatter of rain toward night.

Wednesday, July 1*st.*—Advanced P.M. in pursuit of the enemy, fully equipped, with forty rounds of ammunition and two days' cooked rations per man. Muster-roll of 23d gave 506 officers and men present for duty. 'Column consisted of the 8th, 11th, 23d, 52d, 56th, 68th and 71st N.Y., with section of Miller's Philadelphia Battery;—all under command of Brigadier-General Joseph Knipe. Bivouacked on Trindle Spring Creek, at 10 o'clock, P. M. Weather pleasant. Distance marched, 7 miles.

Thursday, 2*d.*—At 3 A. M., ordered up, and at daylight countermarched two miles. Halted all day. Bivouacked in a cul-de-sac of the Conedoguinet Creek, at a place called Orr's Bridge. Day warm and pleasant. Distance 3 miles.

Frida, 3*d.*—Resumed forward march, disencumbered of knapsacks and woolen blankets. Reached Carlisle at 6 P.M. Afternoon hot and sultry. Distance, 12 miles.

Saturday, 4*th.*—Took Carlisle and Baltimore pike through Papertown and Mt. Holly Gap. Severe storm. At Hunter's Run 23rd, the advance company excepted, countermarched to Mt. Holly paper mill. Crossed the run a little before dark. Regiment arrived at Laurel Forge in detachments during the night, men covered with mud, and exhausted with hunger and fatigue. Distance 17 miles.

Sunday, 5*th.*—At 8 A. M., resumed march. At Pine Grove Iron Works turned to the left and ascended a heavy mountain, on the summit of which halted and bivouacked in support of a masked battery planted at a cross-roads in a grove. Day sultry followed by rainy night. Many of the men without food, and all with but a scanty supply. Distance 5 miles.

Monday, 6*th.* — Rations furnished. About middle of forenoon moved forward. Reached Cashtown, on the Chambersburg and Gettysburg pike, about 8 o'clock. Bivouacked in an orchard. Nothing to eat. Day cloudy and comfortable; roads heavy. Distance 16 miles.

Tuesday, 7*th.*—Ordered to march for Gettysburg, but countermanded. Proceeded in the direction of Chambersburg some seven miles, where took road to Altodale, Pa. Halted near that village about 4 P.M. Day fair; roads heavy; rations distributed. Distance 12 miles.

Wednesday, 8*th.*—Rain set in again about 1 A. M., and soon grew to a furious storm. The whole camp helplessly at its mercy. At 8 A.M., took road again. Marched a little beyond Waynesboro', and formed a junction with Army of Potomac. Day pleasant; roads very heavy. Distance 11 miles.

Thursday, 9*th.*—Rested. Muster rolls of 23rd gave largest number during the campaign, viz: 519 officers and men.

Friday, 10th.—Out for reconnoissance in company with 71st N.Y. Under arms all day in a bare field beneath broiling sun. Returned to camp about dark. Distance 8 miles.

Saturday, 11th.—P. M., column moved toward Hagerstown, the 23rd having the advance. Bivouacked a mile beyond Lettersburg. Company B, 23rd, detailed for picket duty at the front. Evening pleasant. Distance 5 miles.

Sunday, 12th.—Countermarched to Lettersburg where took the Cavetown road, reaching the latter place about noon. Here encountered another terrific thunder storm. Several men of the 56th N.Y., struck by the electric fluid, and one of them killed. Fresh beef rations furnished. Bivouacked in a field which the rain flooded and converted into mire. Roads pretty good and morning comfortable. Distance 9 miles.

Monday, 13th.—Marched toward Boonsboro'. Bivouacked at dark in a rough, stony field, the fires of different encampments of the Army of the Potomac visible in the distance. Rained much through the day; very muddy. Distance 10 miles.

Tuesday, 14th.—Crossed fields to Boonsboro' and Hagerstown pike. Followed it toward the latter to Beaver Creek where encamped. Day pleasant. Distance 5 miles.

Wednesday, 15th.—At 7.30 A.M., started for home, taking the pike for Frederick. Reached Frederick about 6 P. M., and Monocacy Junction about 10 P. M., where encamped in a grove. Weather comfortable; sky overcast most of the day; road dry and pretty smooth, though hard for the feet. A member of the 56th N.Y. fell dead on reaching camp from exhaustion. Distance 25 miles.

Thursday, 16th.—Waiting for transportation.

Friday 17th.—Took cars for Baltimore. Arrived about 4 P. M. Marched to the Philadelphia Depot, and thence to Harrisburg Depot. About midnight took train for the latter city.

Saturday, 18th. — En route for Harrisburg, which we reached about 9 P.M., and at midnight got under way again for Elizabethport, N. J., without change of cars.

Sunday, 19th.—Halted at Easton, Pa., where citizens poured out *en masse* to feed us. Reached Elizabethport shortly after noon, and at once embarked on steamboat for New York. Landed at the Battery, and proceeded directly to the Armory, where were dismissed at 7½ P.M.

Grand total of distances marched during 15 days from July 1st to July 15th inclusive:—ONE HUNDRED AND FORTY-FIVE MILES, or an average of *nine and two-third miles* per day; each man carrying an aggregate of THIRTY POUNDS of luggage, except during the first day's march of *seven miles* in which each carried an aggregate of FORTY-FOUR POUNDS.

Largest number at any roll-call :—FIVE HUNDRED AND NINETEEN, including officers and men.

www.ingramcontent.com/pod-product-compliance
Lightning Source LLC
Chambersburg PA
CBHW030245170426
43202CB00009B/631